Routines-Based Early Intervention Guidebook

A Proven Program for Improving Communication Skills with Activities in English and Spanish

Scott Prath, M.A., CCC-SLP

BILINGUISTICS, INC.
3636 EXECUTIVE CENTER DR., SUITE 268
AUSTIN, TX 78731

Copyright © 2014 Bilinguistics, Inc.
All rights reserved. Printed in the U.S.A.
Previous Edition Copyright © 2008 Bilinguistics, Inc.

Published by Bilinguistics, Inc.
1505 W. Koenig Dr. Austin, TX 78756

For more information, contact Bilinguistics, Inc. or visit us at www.bilinguistics.com.

Permission is granted for the user to print the material contained in this publication. Copies of this material may not be reproduced for entire agencies, used for commercial sale, stored in a retrieval system, or transmitted in any form (electronically, recording, mechanically, web, etc.) without the publisher's explicit permission.

Library of Congress Cataloging-in-Publication Data
ISBN-13: 978-1502856562
ISBN-10: 1502856565

Preface

How it began

This book grew out of the experiences of speech-language pathologists who work with English- and Spanish-speaking families enrolled in early childhood intervention programs in Texas. It utilizes an acronym for five strategies (SMILE—sign, model, imitate, label, and expand) that have been found to improve communication skills in infants and toddlers.

These materials are designed around twelve daily routines where a variety of strategies to increase communication can be used. For example, the "mealtime" routine provides many opportunities to label items and actions, model phrases, imitate sounds, express preferences, and even describe foods. However, each routine also lends itself to teaching a specific strategy (e.g., making requests). At the beginning of every section, we have provided detailed information on a single strategy. By highlighting one strategy in each session, families can more easily learn to incorporate this therapeutic approach into their daily lives.

This program has been field-tested with many families enrolled in early childhood intervention. The children in these families had many different disabilities, including Down Syndrome, Autism, Cerebral Palsy, and general language delays. The families came from different language backgrounds (English, Spanish, and bilingual English/Spanish), and high, middle, and low socioeconomic groups. The generous input and concerns of parents, speech-language pathologists, and early interventionists have strongly influenced the content.

How it has evolved

We have had the opportunity to continue our field-testing of this program and gather additional feedback about its benefits from the families and professionals who use it. Based on their input, we were able to determine how using these strategies assists families in learning ways to help their children develop language skills through everyday events. We have added extra activity ideas that families can easily use at home; pages for children to pull out, cut, color, glue, and paste; and many more signs for interventionists to turn into flashcards.

In addition, we have updated sections on speech and language development to be more concise and useful for interventionists. There is a great section on myths about bilingualism and answers to frequently asked questions to address the concerns of families. There are also more guidelines for interventionists and speech-language pathologists, including a sample treatment session, new data collection sheets, and rationales for working on language development to be shared with families. We also have included more information on speech development and the use of signs as a bridge to developing oral language skills.

ACKNOWLEDGMENTS

The production of this work has been a true team effort, and there are many people to thank for their countless hours of work on this project. First of all, we would like to thank the members of the Bilinguistics Team who developed activities; produced charts, tables, and graphs; photographed signs; researched and edited; and gave invaluable input from their experiences and expertise in every aspect of this book.

>Ellen Kester, Ph.D., CCC-SLP
>Scott Prath, M.A., CCC-SLP
>Kara Anderson, M.A., CCC-SLP
>Anne Alvarez, M.A., CCC-SLP
>Marie Wirka, M.S. CCC-SLP
>Keith Lebel, M.A., CCC-SLP
>Adrianne Arrieta-Morales, M.A., CCC-SLP
>Mary Bauman, M.S., CCC-SLP
>May-Ling Castillo Love, M.A., CCC-SLP
>Rebecca Eagleson, M.A., CCC-SLP
>Alyson Hendry, M.A., CCC-SLP
>Katherine Marting, M.A., CCC-SLP
>Meagan Morgan, M.S., CCC-SLP
>Eva Uribe

We would also like to thank María Crespo for her work in translating text into Spanish and Adriana Lebel for her work with translating, editing, and proofreading.

Special thanks go to Maritza Jacobs for her tireless work on formatting and style.

Finally, we would like to say thank you to you for purchasing the Routines-Based Early Intervention Guidebook. We are thrilled that you have decided to make this comprehensive therapy program an integral part of your service delivery to families. We believe in its success and hope that this will be your experience as well.

Sincerely,

The Bilinguistics Team

TABLE OF CONTENTS

Introduction 1

Collaborating with Caregivers 3

Speech Production 6

Using this Guidebook: A Sample Session 10

Session Record Form 12

Session Plans 13

    Session 1: Daily Routine/La rutina diaria
        Focus: Having a Plan (1) 17
        English (1.1) 18
        Spanish (1.2) 20
        Signs/Señas (1.3) 22
        Data Collection Sheet (1.4) 24

    Session 2: Greetings/Saludos
        Focus: Two-word Utterances (2) 27
        English (2.1) 28
        Spanish (2.2) 30
        Signs/Señas (2.3) 32
        Teaching Two-word Utterances (2.4) 34

    Session 3: Mealtime/La hora de comer
        Focus: Requests (3) 41
        English (3.1) 42
        Spanish (3.2) 44
        Signs/Señas (3.3) 46
        Teaching How to Make Requests (3.4) 48

    Session 4: Getting Dressed/Vestirse
        Focus: Expanding Phrases (4) 55
        English (4.1) 56
        Spanish (4.2) 58
        Signs/Señas (4.3) 60
        Teaching How to Expand Phrases (4.4) 62

Table of Contents

Session 5: Toys and Playtime/Jugando
    Focus: Turn-Taking (5) 67
    English (5.1) 68
    Spanish (5.2) 70
    Signs/Señas (5.3) 72
    Teaching How to Take Turns (5.4) 74

Session 6: Outside/Afuera
    Focus: Change of State—Identifying Emotions (6) 81
    English (6.1) 82
    Spanish (6.2) 84
    Signs/Señas (6.3) 86
    Teaching How to Identify Emotions (6.4) 88

Session 7: In the Car/En el carro
    Focus: Describing (7) 95
    English (7.1) 96
    Spanish (7.2) 98
    Signs/Señas (7.3) 100
    Teaching How to Describe (7.4) 102

Session 8: Shopping/Ir de compras
    Focus: Categorization (8) 109
    English (8.1) 110
    Spanish (8.2) 112
    Signs/Señas (8.3) 114
    Teaching Categorization Skills (8.4) 116

Session 9: At Home/En la casa
    Focus: Labeling (9) 123
    English (9.1) 124
    Spanish (9.2) 126
    Signs/Señas (9.3) 128
    Teaching Labeling Skills (9.4) 130

Session 10: Bathtime/Bañarse
    Focus: Imitation (10) 137
    English (10.1) 138
    Spanish (10.2) 140
    Signs/Señas (10.3) 142
    Teaching How to Imitate (10.4) 144

Table of Contents

Session 11: Storytime/Tiempo de leer
    Focus: Contrasting (11) 151
    English (11.1) 152
    Spanish (11.2) 154
    Signs/Señas (11.3) 156
    Teaching Contrasting Skills (11.4) 158

Session 12: Bedtime/Acostarse
    Focus: Following Directions (12) 165
    English (12.1) 166
    Spanish (12.2) 168
    Signs/Señas (12.3) 170
    Teaching How to Follow Directions (12.4) 172

Appendix
    FACT or MYTH? FAQs about Bilingual Language Development 177
    Apples to Apples Chart 178
    SMILE Strategies for Speech Production 179
    Speech Development 180
    Phonological Development 182
    Typical Phonological Processes 183
    Language Milestones 184

Indices of Signs/Índices de señas
    English 186
    Spanish 188

References 190

INTRODUCTION

This guidebook was developed by a group of bilingual speech-language pathologists who have provided therapy services to young children and their families through home-based early childhood intervention programs. The goal of many early childhood intervention programs is to help families to work with their children by incorporating language strategies into their daily routines. In this model, it is not uncommon for the speech-language pathologist to see a family only one or two times per month. While this paradigm works well for a handful of families, we found that many families did not continue to work on the activities and strategies that were suggested between therapy sessions. By talking with the families, we learned that it was not that they did not want to carry out the activities, but that they could not remember all of the strategies, signs, and other information their therapist shared with them, and they did not always know the rationale for using them. While we use these strategies every day with the children and families we work with, this information is new to most of them. Parents benefit from having materials to work with and to serve as reminders of strategies targeted during therapy.

The content of this program was driven by theory and research in the fields of child development, communication development, and early intervention. The lessons and activities in this book are based on Vygotsky's (1967) social learning theories. Social learning theories view social interaction as critical to development. Therefore, the family members involved in early childhood intervention programs are seen as the child's guides, and the child is the apprentice who learns from the adult models (Rogoff, 1990). Every strategy and every activity in this book incorporate the family members as important social interactionists and as key models of communicative behaviors.

Some very simple principles from theory and research have been incorporated. Frequency and consistency are two of those principles. Simply put, the more a child hears a word or phrase, the more likely he or she is to use that phrase. Secondly, the more consistently a word or phrase achieves the desired outcome, the more likely a child is to use it. Strategies that drive these two principles include modeling and imitating. These are very simple ideas that can produce great change when used frequently and consistently.

Another key component of this guidebook's success is the use of sign language. Many parents of children with communication delays and disorders become very concerned when a speech-language pathologist proposes the use of sign language. When probed further about their concerns, many parents have reported that they are afraid their children will learn to sign and not learn to talk, or that they will no longer be motivated to learn to speak if they can communicate with sign language. Current literature suggests that the use of sign with children leads to earlier and clearer parent-child communication, accelerated spoken language development, reduced crying and whining, improved parent-child bonding, and increased intelligence (Goodwyn, Acredolo, & Brown, 2000; Thompson et al., 2007). Additionally, Pizer, Walters, & Meier (2007) found that families of children who learned signs to communicate stopped using signs when children began to communicate well orally (around 2 years of age).

While parents may be resistant to the use of signs to help their children develop early language skills, sharing data about sign use with families may ease concerns and help increase family participation.

Increasing family participation in therapy increases children's success in communication. The tricky part is how to do it. Obviously, this will vary somewhat from family to family, but there are a few strategies that have been indicated in the research to increase family participation. First, it is important that we share with families *why* we are suggesting these changes in how they interact with their child. Families are much more likely to use suggested strategies if they know *why* therapists suggest them. A recent study of Mexican immigrant mothers' perceptions of their children's intervention (Kummerer, Lopez-Deyna & Hughes, 2007) found that most of the mothers in the study felt that therapists were just playing with their children. By helping families recognize the important role of play in development, families are more likely to see play as a way to incorporate new language strategies. Additionally, teaching how individual cognitive skills contribute to language development, such as understanding that objects still exist when they are out of sight, will encourage families to work on those cognitive skills in play.

Incorporating therapeutic strategies into the routines of each family and using toys and household items in the child's environment have also been found to be effective for increasing family participation and their use of intervention strategies. Home-based service providers often bring in a bag of toys filled with excellent intervention tools. They then pack up the toys and leave with the expectation that families will carry through with all of the suggestions. McWilliams (2007) found that families often attribute their children's progress to people outside of the family (and maybe their toys) rather than to regular interactions within the family. Many early childhood intervention programs have encouraged therapists to make use of what is in each family's home. This program does this by providing numerous ideas on how to use household objects to improve communication.

This book is structured to capitalize on the use of everyday routines and household objects to increase communication skills. Each lesson is easy to use and easily adapted to each and every individual family. Each family can be provided with their own handouts that allow parents to keep track of their child's progress, record activities, and remind them of signs and important vocabulary words. The parent handouts also provide information about typical language and speech development, and references for the strategies they are beginning to incorporate into their daily routines. The families we have worked with have been very pleased to have such important information at their fingertips, and we have found that the families who retain written activity suggestions have been much more engaged in the intervention process than those who have not had comparable information.

COLLABORATING WITH CAREGIVERS

We want the best for the children we work with.

As speech-language pathologists working in a variety of settings, we have had the opportunity to team with caregivers of all types in implementing intervention for young children with communication difficulties. While searching for the "best way" to do so, we have come to realize that we can achieve a kind of *synergy* when we fully involve parents and caregivers. Synergy, by definition, is when one or more components are combined to create a product that is even greater than the effects they would have if they were added up individually. Simply put, teaming with parents and caregivers gives you the most bang for your buck. Better progress is seen at a faster rate.

How do we collaborate with caregivers?

How do we ensure that caregivers understand *what* they can do, *how* they can do it, and *why* they should do it? It is almost always the case that they *want* to help; that is rarely a problem. In order to have successful collaboration, we have to explain the *what*, the *how*, and the *why* of communication intervention. Before we can do this, we first have to determine how the caregivers view and understand their children's communication behaviors, and what they know about helping their children improve their communication skills. In other words, we need to *assess the caregivers*. This is done by posing open-ended questions in order to provide families with an opportunity to tell their story. By listening to them and observing their interactions with their children, we gain valuable information about how to approach collaboration. After making this initial assessment, our next step is to provide them with the knowledge and tools that we use as professionals to help their children improve their communication skills. By doing so, we effectively enable caregivers to become the interventionists!

How do we encourage 'buy-in' from families

1. Package up our ideas and present them in a way that makes sense.
The first thing we can do is assure parents and caregivers that they are not the reason their child has difficulty communicating, as well as provide positive reinforcement for their efforts to help their child. Parenting is not easy, and parenting a child who requires special care presents an added challenge.

2. Avoid making assumptions.
Whether you are a speech-language pathologist, early interventionist, or other professional, you likely have immersed yourself in a discipline that comes with a specific knowledge base, terminology and perspective. To work with caregivers, you need to step outside of your world, throw your acronyms out of the window, and start from the beginning. The 'beginning' is usually different for each caregiver.

3. Remember that collaboration is a process.

When you learned about your discipline, even if you were immersed and bombarded with information, your actual understanding and skills were formed across many months, even years. Collaboration is not a 'one-time thing.' It requires patience, empathy, and a true commitment. As you can see, it involves many of the qualities we use when working with the children themselves!

4. Take risks.

We are accustomed to teaching children. We give them instructions with great ease and comfort. We ask them to do things without hesitation. In working with caregivers, the nuance of achieving a working relationship varies based on personalities, cultural factors, and learning styles. Regardless, it requires some level of confidence in the value of what you know and do, and the importance of sharing your ideas with other adults. Invariably, this requires some level of risk-taking. Do it. Be up-front with people. Tell them that we will try things together, some of which will work better than others. We take risks together as a team. Change requires trying new things and taking risks.

Now, it's time to get to work. Let's look at one speech-language pathologist's experience with "Juan."

> Juan was referred for a speech and language evaluation when he was 2 years, 7 months old. He was using approximately 12 words. He was also fairly defiant, easily frustrated, and had reduced attention and play skills. I had the pleasure of collaborating with his mother, who voiced frustration and concern at the outset of therapy. His mother had been doing her best to work with Juan, and was observed trying to have him repeat words, sometimes while withholding objects. As could be expected for anyone without specialized training in communication intervention, her use of strategies and specific cues with Juan was limited.
>
> *Enter: the Routines-Based Early Intervention Guidebook*
>
> I worked with Juan's mother on the basics of communication intervention (i.e., the WHAT and HOW) before telling her WHY. I praised her for her efforts and explained to her that, together, we would explore some 'tricks' (e.g., strategies, cueing) that often work with speech- and language-impaired children. I explained that the 'tricks' that I use are neither secret (gasp!) nor extremely difficult (bigger gasp!). Then I provided an overview of the program and what we are going to do over the following weeks. It sounded something like this:
>
> *"I understand that you would like us to work together to help Juan with his communication skills. I am excited to help you because I have some new ideas and 'tricks,' or strategies, that we can try together to help him communicate*

better. The strategies we use in speech therapy can be used by anyone who wants to help Juan.

I can imagine that beginning this process could seem overwhelming. How are you supposed to find time to use strategies to help Juan communicate into your daily life? As we move forward, we'll work together to identify the most appropriate words to try (i.e., targets) and how to try them (i.e., cues, strategies). We'll do this while having fun and using our tips and 'tricks' during routines that are already a part of your day. This is ideal because it means that there is no 'extra' work for us, there are lots of natural opportunities for practice, and the words that Juan learns will be very useful in his daily routines. This will also help him be less frustrated. Let me show you this great tool that we can use to guide us as we work on all of this together.

We know that certain things help children increase their communication skills. For example, we know that helping them to 'see' sounds, syllables, and words (i.e., using visual cues) is helpful. We know that imitating movements (i.e., using motor/tactile cues) can also help them to use words. We also know that the part of the brain that controls the mouth is next to the part of the brain that controls the hands. This means that, if we use the hands, it often encourages movement of the mouth. Since Juan is currently frustrated when he tries to talk, we should think about giving him ways to communicate that are easier than trying to say words. Using gestures and sign language are great ways to temporarily provide Juan with a communication system that will allow you to know what he wants and needs and be a bridge to oral speech and language development. We will do this by saying words aloud when we use the signs. But wait! Why are we using signs if we want Juan to talk? Research shows us that children who sign begin to talk more, provided they have the physical ability to do so, which we have already determined that Juan does have. Research also tells us that once a child is able to communicate a word with their mouth instead of their hands, they do. So this will be something we will use as a tool to get him talking more.

Let's also have a look at some of the other strategies: modeling, imitation, labeling, and expansion . . ."

This introduction to the research-based techniques and strategies that are contained within this book is just the beginning. Each strategy should be given the time and attention that is needed to help caregivers feel comfortable using them in a natural, functional, and focused way. As we go through this process, we can ensure successful collaboration by remembering that ultimately, in addition to improving children's communication skills, our goal is to help families improve all on their own.

Speech Production

What is speech production?

Speech production, also commonly referred to as articulation, can be simply stated as the ability to form sounds. When children have difficulty making the sounds that are typical for their age, we need to use strategies to facilitate speech production.

How does speech production begin?

Overall, the ability to produce sounds follows a predictable path. It is cumulative and builds upon itself. The following is a broad view of speech development from birth. Tables and charts with developmental milestones in speech production can also be found in the Appendix of this book.

Speech production begins at birth. Children start out by making simple, involuntary (unintentional) noises, such as crying, 'cooing,' laughing, and squealing. Then, they progress to making more complex, voluntary (purposeful) sounds with their mouths. At approximately 6 months of age, they begin to babble, and by about 8-12 months of age their productions begin to sound more and more like adult speech. Within this period of development, children play with sounds. They imitate animal sounds and environmental noises, as well as the speech that they hear from the adults in their world.

As the speech production system develops, both physiologically (nature) and through feedback from caregivers (nurture), our *expectations* about speech production have to evolve. A great illustration of this is the important transition caregivers need to make from responding to the child's cry in the first year of life, to responding to the child's first words by 12-18 months. Caregivers need to tune into their child. This means they always have a mental list of where the child is in development and what the appropriate expectations are. Expectations need to align with abilities, if not, the result is frustration.

When first words appear, they are usually one or two syllables in length (i.e., ba/ball, mama/mom). As the child's first 50 words develop, it is common to repeat the same syllable two times (e.g., bye-bye, night-night). Children tend to use certain sounds before other sounds. Early sounds are often sounds that are produced with the lips and the tip of the tongue including: b, p, m, d, t, and n. It is important that the words and sounds we choose to target follow these developmental patterns.

As children's words develop, they become more similar to adult pronunciation. Children also begin to combine words into short phrases and sentences. The words we choose to target at this stage should continue to follow developmental patterns. We begin to shape the one- to two-syllable words that the child is already using into longer three- and four-syllable words or phrases. For example, if the child is producing "nana," a logical next step might be for him to produce "<u>ba</u>nana." This could also be targeted in phrases by combining the child's words with one other simple word. For example, if the child is already saying the word "*mi*" (my), we could target phrase such as "mi mamá" (my mommy) or "mi bebé" (my baby). Again, this is about building and shaping speech production skills. Sudden jumps in complexity that are too far from the child's current abilities can often be met with frustration.

What are speech production difficulties?

When children's difficulties with speech production are more severe, this process of slowly building and shaping the child's productions by following developmental patterns becomes even more crucial. Children whose speech production differs from their peers are either *delayed* in their speech production or have *atypical* speech production abilities. *Delayed speech production* implies that children are following the same developmental course as children with typical development but at a later age. In other words, they produce earlier sounds, such as "b" and "m," before later sounds, such as "r" and "l." Children with *atypical speech production* do not follow a typical developmental sequence. For example, children with cleft lip and palate do not acquire oral plosive sounds (i.e., "p" and "b") early in development as a result of structural abnormalities. The type of speech production difficulty a child has requires careful attention to which targets we choose, and how we work on those targets.

Included in every session, there is a section called "My Child Will," where the interventionist and family can state their goal for the child in terms of speech and/or language production. When children need speech production difficulties to be addressed more specifically, this can be done through the use of speech bubbles that are labeled "Therapist Suggests." In this space, the speech-language pathologist can make suggestions for additional *cueing* or *modeling* strategies to help children improve in this area as well. Examples of how to integrate these strategies within the SMILE framework are also available in the Appendix of this book.

What strategies can we use to facilitate speech production?

Cueing:

We often use *multisensory cueing*. This is a technical term for helping the child produce sounds by incorporating the use of many of their senses. Specifically, we use visual, tactile, motor, and auditory cues. The goal is to gradually fade these cues as the child becomes more successful in producing the target sound. Below we discuss each of the multisensory cues. These cues are often used simultaneously.

- <u>Visual cues</u> may include demonstrating placement through exaggerated mouth movements, calling attention to the mouth or face with hand signals, and/or providing pictures (e.g., having children simultaneously point to two dots as they say a word with two parts, such as "ga-to"/cat). A mirror will allow children to see their own mouths as they produce sounds, which provides a connection between the way sounds look and feel.

- <u>Tactile/touch cues</u> may include physically touching and manipulating the child's face, jaw, lips, and tongue in order to show them the correct placement for specific sounds, or using touch to draw attention to certain sounds and their characteristics. For example, pointing to your nose to cue for sounds where the air goes through the nose (i.e., m, n) or dragging your finger along the child's arm while saying a long sound like "s," as opposed to a short sound like "d."

- <u>Motor/movement cues</u> may include the use of large, or gross motor cues such as jumping, stomping, waving, tapping, and/or clapping the sounds or syllables of a word as well as small, or fine motor cues such as finger tapping or pointing.

- <u>Auditory/sound cues</u> may include emphasizing a particular sound in a word (e.g., "mmm, mama") or in the child's environment (e.g., "shhh," the sound of water while taking a bath) as well as providing melodic cues, which use music, rhythm, or song-like productions to draw attention to certain sounds or syllables.

Modeling:

In addition to the use of cues, speech production is also facilitated through providing models of the targeted sounds. Modeling involves giving children a slow, clear, and deliberate example of the sound or word they are attempting to produce.

Tips for modeling appropriate speech production:

- It is natural to provide one model for the child in order to demonstrate how to correctly produce a sound. For example, if the child says "dat," our response is "yes, it's a cat." However, to be even more effective as a model, you should repeat the correct production several times without interrupting the natural flow of the conversation (e.g., "Yes, it's a <u>cat</u>. It's a yellow <u>cat</u>. The <u>cat</u> is sleeping").

- When providing a model, we draw the child's attention to the missing or incorrect sound by emphasizing the sound in our model. One way of doing this is by repeating the initial sound of the word (e.g., papa, p, p, p). We can also break groups of sounds (clusters) apart and say them separately (e.g., cream becomes "c"-"ream") and then repeat the whole word (e.g., "cream").

- Many children automatically simplify adult words by using *phonological processes*. However, some children may require that the adult simplify the target word for them.

For example, "Does baby want a nana (banana)?" can be said slowly and with extra emphasis.

- When the child is able to produce the sounds and words correctly, you can encourage him or her to repeat the correct production either immediately after you (e.g., The adult says, "Say 'cat.'") or with a delay (e.g., The adult says, "Up, up, up. Where is the truck going?" and the child says, "Up.").

- The target sound can also be elicited without providing a direct model. With this method, the adult begins a familiar phrase that contains a sound the child is practicing and the child finishes it. For example, the adult might say "Ready, set..." and the child says, "Go!"

A few reminders:

- *Don't overlook the obvious.* Sometimes children need help learning to use intentional vocalizations before working on higher level skills. For example, the child's use of any vowel or sound attempt (such as "ah") should be reinforced with a response from the adult. You don't always begin at the word level.

- The more significant the speech production problem, the greater the importance of *careful target selection.* Choose targets that include at least one sound the child can produce.

- *Cover all your bases.* Teach the caregiver how to use multiple cues simultaneously, and also how to choose appropriate targets.

Remember Juan?

We started using play food as a therapy material. The complexity of the targets varied widely. We needed to carefully choose easy targets to build Juan's skills and confidence, and reduce his frustration. We combined the SIGN for 'eat' with *multiple cueing strategies* (see above) while targeting words with *simple sounds* such as the "p" in "pan" (Spanish for "bread") and "apple."

Then we developed appropriate *expectations* based on his abilities and developmental milestones. Our goal was that he would at least vocalize with the purpose of requesting the food or use his own form of the word such as "pa" for "pan." All of this was taught to his mother who learned to actively give cues and models and choose targets after Juan had learned that his use of sounds had a *purpose*.

Using this Guidebook

A Sample Session

A program is successful when there is long-term planning, consistency across sessions, and progress monitoring. Collecting baseline data in the first session and additional data in each subsequent session is central to this process. In the first session the interventionist and the caregiver should work together to complete the baseline Data Collection Sheet found at the end of Session 1: Daily Routine/La Rutina Diaria (1.4). Together they can select one daily routine on which to focus and record detailed information that can be used to monitor the child's growth in receptive and expressive language skills from the beginning to the end of the program. This sheet can also be reproduced to collect baseline data for additional daily routines that are used throughout the program. A Data Collection Sheet should be kept for each routine that is presented and should take no more than a few minutes of each session to update.

This program allows the interventionist and caregivers the flexibility to determine which strategies and daily routines they will use in the order that is most relevant to the family and the child. The rest of the daily routines do not have to be used in any specific order after Session 1. The interventionist can then demonstrate use of the strategy for the caregivers within the daily routine and allow them an opportunity to practice it themselves. This will lead to a discussion of *what* the strategy is, *how* to use it within the context of the daily routine, and *why* it will be helpful for their child. The interventionist and caregiver can select daily routines, important words, and strategies on which they would like to focus. The Session Record Form can be used to keep track of the routines and strategies that are used with the child, as well as the goal for each session, and the results that are reported by parents at the beginning of the following session. In addition, within each daily routine there is a page with activity ideas that also serves as a tool for progress monitoring and can be employed to:

- Record which of the SMILE strategies the caregivers will use to help the child between sessions.
- Determine what new goals, words, and communication skills the caregivers would like the child to accomplish.
- Provide additional suggestions for improving speech production through cueing or modeling strategies.
- Serve as 'homework' for the caregivers to complete between visits and show to the therapist in the following session.
- Make additional notes about what the caregivers did to help the child, how the child responded, and what questions the caregivers have about using the strategy.

On the following page is an example of a therapy session with a sample script. Additional copies can be printed for free at www.bilinguistics.com

Time	Activity	A Sample Script
9:00-9:05	Review the plan for the session with the family.	First, we are going to review the strategies you have used with your child and talk about how he/she responded. We will discuss which strategies we want to focus on today and demonstrate how to implement them. Then you will have an opportunity to practice using the strategy with your child. At the end of the session, we will make a plan for you to implement the strategy in daily routines with your child.
9:05-9:15	Review of progress: clinician will take data on strategy used and progress/no progress observed.	Have there been any medical updates or changes in the family since our last visit (e.g., hearing eval, pediatrician visit, etc.)? How did your child do this week? Let's update the Data Collection Sheet with the new words that your child uses and understands. What strategies did you use and how did he/she respond? Can you describe how you used **modeling** during the bath routine? Let's look at the progress you noted in your parent handbook.
9:15-9:20	Choose the daily routine, and important words and strategy to focus on. Write it in each corresponding section.	Okay, would you like to continue with **modeling** or are you ready to try a new strategy? You are doing a great job **modeling** during the bath routine. Let's try to use **expansion** to increase your child's use of verbs. Let's choose a few important verbs to focus on this week. I will write them in your parent handbook. During which daily routine would you like to try **expansion**? Mealtime or playtime?
9:20-9:40	Demonstrate the use of the strategy and give the family opportunities to practice using the strategy in different activities.	First, I will model how I **expand** on your child's utterances, then we will switch and you will practice using the **expansion** strategy.
9:40-9:45*	Write up the note and review with parents.	Today, we have reviewed your child's progress, chosen a new strategy, practiced using the new strategy, and have set a goal for your next session. I would like you to use the strategy in at least three different settings and keep track of how your child responds in your parent handbook. Great job, I will see you next week at 9:00 a.m.

Example is based on a 45-minute home visit.

SESSION RECORD FORM

Child's Name_____ Date of Birth: _____

DATE	ROUTINE	STRATEGY	CHILD'S GOAL	RESULTS

BILINGUISTICS

Session Plans

Session 1

Daily Routine

La rutina diaria

Daily Routine

Speech and Language Session Focus

Having a Plan

Service providers and parents alike find it challenging to create consistent changes in the home so that a child's communication improves. The service provider works to encourage change, but often returns for the next family visit to find that suggestions did not work or were not carried out.

Meanwhile, parents become excited by success during sessions but have difficulty replicating these behaviors when working with their child alone. Success in home-based intervention is dependent on parents taking the communication strategies that lead to success and using them on a daily basis.

The purpose of the introductory session is to let the parent know that we have a plan, it is long-term, and that we are on the same team. During this session, it is important to communicate to the parent that:

- We understand how busy they are and we will add nothing to their day, only make each event more language-rich.
- We understand how difficult it is to have a child with a delay or disorder, and will be working with them and remain a consistent resource.
- For a successful program, both the parent and the interventionist will have to work to increase the child's communication.
- Both parties need to note what works and what does not. *This feedback is the only way we are going to make consistent progress.*

Today's Plan

- Talk about the different daily routines and write down how the child communicates during each routine.
- Have the parents identify which routines are most important to the family.
- Identify frustrating situations and address them during the next session.

Daily Routine

1.1

Sign	Use signs and words together. **More** **Please** **All Done**
Model	Use simple phrases. **"Hi, Dad"** **"More milk please"**
Imitate	Imitate sounds, signs, words, and gestures that your child uses. **Imitate saying "Hello" and "Bye-bye."**
Label	Name objects in your child's environment. **"Car" "Ball"**
Expand	Add words to what your child says. **When your child says "Hi," you say, "Hi, Mom."**

Practice these important words and add more of your own:

HI	PLAY	_____
CHILD'S NAME	EAT	_____
ME	PLEASE	_____
YOU	HELP	_____
MORE	ALL DONE	_____

DAILY ROUTINE

ACTIVITY IDEAS:
- Make a list of activities that your child is engaged in when he/she talks the most.

- Notice what you do naturally to help your child to talk: repeating words, singing, naming toys/pictures.

- Write down how your child lets you know he/she is hungry, tired, is "all done," etc.

I will help my child by:

- _____
- _____

My child will:

_____
_____
_____
_____

THERAPIST SUGGESTS:

What happened?

-What did you do?
-What did your child say or do?
-What questions do you have?

_____
_____
_____
_____

La Rutina Diaria

1.2

SEÑALAR	Junte señas y palabras. **Más Por favor Se acabó**
OFRECER **M**ODELOS	Diga frases sencillas. **"Hola, papá" "Más leche por favor"**
NOMBRAR	Nombre objetos en su ambiente. **"Carro" "Pelota"**
REPETIR **Í**MITAR	Repita sonidos, señas, palabras, y gestos que usa su niño/a. **Repita "Hola" y "Adiós."**
EXTENDER	Añada palabras a lo que dice su niño/a. **Cuando su niño/a diga "Hola," usted dígale,"Hola, Mamá."**

Practiquen estas palabras importantes y agreguen más:

HOLA	JUGAR	_____
NOMBRE del NIÑO/A	COMER	_____
MÍ	POR FAVOR	_____
TÚ	AYUDA	_____
MÁS	SE ACABÓ	_____

La Rutina Diaria

IDEAS DE ACTIVIDADES:

- Haga una lista de las actividades que su niño/a disfruta, para averiguar con cual habla más.

- Observe lo que Ud. hace normalmente para ayudar a hablar a su niño/a: repetir palabras, cantar, decir el nombre de juguetes o imágenes.

- Anote como su niño/a le comunica que tiene hambre, que está cansado, que ha terminado, etc.

Ayudaré a mi niño/a así:

- _____
- _____

Mi niño/a va a:

_____
_____
_____

Sugerencia de la Terapista:

¿Qué pasó?

- ¿Qué hizo Ud.?
- ¿Qué dijo o hizo su niño/a?
- ¿Qué preguntas tiene Ud.?

_____
_____
_____

Daily Routine/La Rutina Diaria 1.3

Signs/Señas

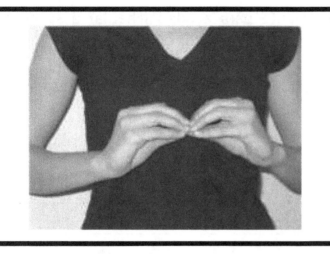

More / Más

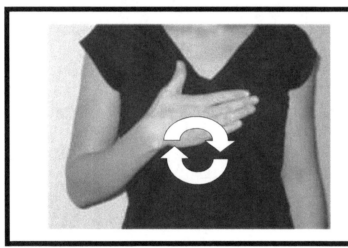

Please / Por favor

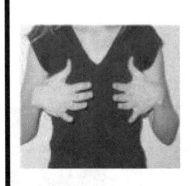 

All done / Se acabó

Daily Routine/La Rutina Diaria

Routines-Based Early Intervention Guidebook

Daily Routine/La Rutina Diaria 1.4

Data Collection Sheet

Child's Name: _____ Date of Birth: _____

Daily Routine/La Rutina Diaria: _____

Date / Fecha	What words or gestures does your child use? / ¿Cuáles palabras o gestos de mano usa su niño/a?	What words or activities does your child understand? / ¿Cuáles palabras o actividades entiende su niño/a?

Date / Fecha	What words or gestures does your child use? / ¿Cuáles palabras o gestos de mano usa su niño/a?	What words or activities does your child understand? / ¿Cuáles palabras o actividades entiende su niño/a?

BILINGUISTICS

This page may be reproduced for working with children as part of the SMILE program.

Session 2

Greetings

Saludos

GREETINGS 2

SPEECH AND LANGUAGE SESSION FOCUS

TWO-WORD UTTERANCES

Acknowledgement is an important bond between a parent and a child. This natural need to interact with each other creates a motivational opportunity to use two words together. This can be as simple as a greeting (e.g., "Hi," "Bye," "High five") paired with a family member's name. Or, a child can be possessive of his or her parent and announce, "My Daddy," to show his or her excitement.

The transition between one-word utterances and two-word utterances is often difficult and can take a long time. Two-word utterances are most easily borne out of the combination of two words that the child already uses. Greetings and family member names happen to comprise two of the highest-frequency word groups across all languages.

TODAY'S PLAN

Parents should be encouraged to:

- Have their child greet family and visitors every time they come home or leave.
- Request a physical interaction such as a high five, hand shake, or hug.
- Say the parent's name and/or child's name along with the physical interaction, such as "Give me five, (child's name)!"
- Identify a greeting that is extremely fun for the child so that he/she looks forward to it. For example, a parent can swing the child around when they greet each other, run from them playfully, or have a secret hand shake.

GREETINGS

2.1

SIGN	Use signs and words together. **Mom Dad Where**
MODEL	Use simple phrases. **"Bye, Dad" "Let's play"**
IMITATE	Imitate sounds, signs, words, and gestures that your child uses. **Imitate waving "Hello" and "Bye-bye."**
LABEL	Name objects in your child's environment. **"Uncle" "Grandma"**
EXPAND	Add words to what your child says. **When your child says "Daddy," you say, "Your Daddy."**

Practice these important words and add more of your own:

HELLO	COUSIN	_____
MOM	BYE-BYE	_____
DAD	HOUSE	_____
BROTHER/SISTER	WHERE	_____
UNCLE/AUNT	GRANDPA/GRANDMA	_____

GREETINGS

ACTIVITY IDEAS:
- Label family members by name while pointing to photos. Encourage imitation of pointing and labeling.

- Glue pictures of family members to popsicle sticks. Pull them out of a bag to practice saying "Hi" (e.g., "Hi, Grandma") and put them back into the bag to practice saying "Bye" (e.g., "Bye, Mom").

- Sing the song "Hello (child's name)" to the tune of Frère Jacques.

I will help my child by:

- _____
- _____

My child will:

_____
_____
_____
_____

THERAPIST SUGGESTS:

What happened?

-What did you do?
-What did your child say or do?
-What questions do you have?

_____
_____
_____
_____

SALUDOS

2.2

SEÑALAR	Junte señas y palabras. **La mamá El papá Dónde**
OFRECER **M**ODELOS	Diga frases sencillas. **"Adiós, Papá" "Juguemos afuera"**
NOMBRAR	Nombre objetos en su ambiente. **"Tío" "Abuelita"**
REPETIR	Repita sonidos, señas, palabras, y gestos que usa su niño/a. **Imite saludando "Hola" y "Adiós."**
ÍMITAR	
EXTENDER	Añada palabras a lo que dice su niño/a. **Cuando su niño/a diga "Adiós," usted dígale, "Adiós, abuela."**

Practiquen estas palabras importantes y agreguen más:

HOLA	PRIMO/A	_____
MAMÁ	ADIÓS	_____
PAPÁ	LA CASA	_____
HERMANO/A	DÓNDE	_____
TÍO/A	ABUELO/A	_____

SALUDOS

IDEAS DE ACTIVIDADES:
- Diga los nombres de los miembros de la familia mientras los señala en fotografías. Estimule a su niño/a para que imite señalarlos y nombrarlos.

- Pegue fotos de miembros de la familia en palitos de helados. Sáquelos de una bolsa para practicar decir "hola" (por ejemplo, "Hola, abuela") y vuelva a meterlos en la bolsa para practicar decir "adios" (por ejemplo, "Adiós, mamá").

- Cante la canción "Hola (el nombre de su niño/a)" con la melodía de "Las Manitos."

Ayudaré a mi niño/a así:

- _____
- _____

Mi niño/a va a:

_____
_____
_____
_____

SUGERENCIA DE LA TERAPISTA:

¿Qué pasó?
- ¿Qué hizo Ud.?
- ¿Qué dijo o hizo su niño/a?
- ¿Qué preguntas tiene Ud.?

_____
_____
_____
_____

Greetings/Saludos

Signs/Señas

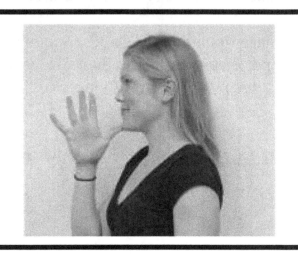

Mom

Mamá

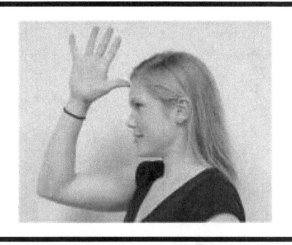

Dad

Papá

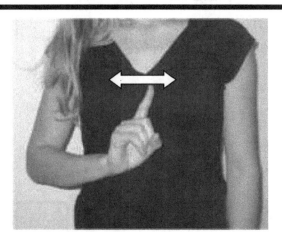

Where

Dónde

Greetings/Saludos

Teaching Two-Word Utterances 2.4

Most children start to combine words into two-word utterances between 18 months and 2 years of age. This is also about the time that children begin to understand relationships between objects and actions in their environments. They usually have approximately 50 words in their repertoire when they start to combine words, and their word combinations pull from those words. It's important that when we are encouraging the use of two-word utterances, we use words that your child already knows and is able to use.

What are Two-Word Utterances?

Plainly speaking, two-word utterances are just that—two words together. However, children begin to build two-word utterances by combining two words that they already know or by using one word that occurs very frequently in the child's environment (e.g. my, your, Hi, Daddy...). Here are some examples of two-word utterance targets:

1. Name + Request: mommy more
2. Possessive Pronoun + Object: my bottle
3. Action + Object: drink milk
4. Name + Greeting: Hi Daddy

Taking inventory: What words does your child say?

Often, we believe that a child isn't saying two words together but when we stop to take inventory, we find a large variety of utterances. Get out a recorder or pencil and paper and interact with the child. What we are looking for is a pattern. For example. Does the child always say, "Uuuh," pull on your arm, and say "milk?" Our job is to find that pattern and then use what the child is already doing to get a variety of utterances such as:

"Uuuh," pulls on your arm, and says "play"

"Uuuh," pulls on your arm, and says "cracker"

Remember, gestures such as pulling and pointing *are* "words" for now. We will replace them with words eventually but for now we just want our child to use more than one word.

TEACHING TWO-WORD UTTERANCES

How to Work with a Child to Produce Two-Word Utterances

Here are a variety of examples to fit your life and schedule. Language does not occur in a vacuum. You will have the most success if you change daily situations to be more language rich rather than adding time to your day to practice communication.

Modeling

Put two words together at the child's level and have him or her repeat you.

1. Provide an example of the two words together.

2. Create an utterance that is a sign + word (e.g. waving bye and saying, "Daddy")

3. Break down the phrase: Have a child who cannot produce two-words together? Say each word individually and have the child repeat the word.

    Adult: "Goodbye, Sammy"

    Child: No response

    Adult: "Goodbye" + wave

    Child: "Goodbye"

    Adult: "Sammy"

    Child: "Sammy"

    Adult: "Awesome! You said, 'Goodbye, Sammy.'"

Book–Reading Activities

Book-reading is a great way to break language down into two-word phrases while the child has a visual representation of the two words. This can refer to the written two words or the picture that represents the two words (red scarf, 2 birds). Any book can be used for this activity. Books that are highly successful combine DESCRIPTION + OBJECT NAME such as *One Fish Two Fish* or *Blue Cat*." This website also has a great list of books: The Speech Bookshelf.com. You can find lists of great books to use with children at: www.bilinguistics.com/books-for-speech-therapy/

Routines-Based Early Intervention Guidebook

Teaching Two-Word Utterances 2.4

Physical activities

Our little guys are HIGHLY active. Let's use this to our advantage and get them jumping, running and laughing their way into two-word utterances. The trick is to have the continuation of the activity depend on their production of two-words. For example, in order to continue jumping, get the ball kicked to them, or get more Playdoh, they produce two words or a word combined with the sign for MORE or PLEASE. Here are some examples of how almost any physical activity can be used to expand utterances.

1. Bubble popping: my turn, more bubbles
2. Building a tower: more blocks, went boom, size + what to make—big house
3. Jumping: I jump, you jump
4. Ball throwing: your turn
5. Stacking cups: one cup, two cups, red cup, cup please
6. Playdoh: want + shape/color
7. Knock Knock—Have a person practice greetings by going out of the room with stuffed animals. They say, "Who is it?" Child has to say "Hi" + animal. Then move on to the next.

School Activities

Utterances can be expanded throughout the day through a system of "laddering." Laddering is basically accepting what the child says and going up one rung in difficulty by giving them an example of what a bigger phrase sounds like. While it is a good idea to have the child produce the new phrase, he doesn't have to. Laddering is different that regular utterance expansion because it is child-initiated and always spontaneous.

Child: "Doggy"

Adult: "Yes, big brown doggy"

Can stop here or:

Adult: "Say: big brown doggy"

Child: "Brown doggy"

Adult: "Great job, you said brown doggy!"

Two-Word Utterance Activity
Greetings/Saludos

Draw or glue pictures of the members of your family into the picture frame. Count and name them. Use the two-word phrase MY + FAMILY MEMBER.

Dibuje o pegue fotos de los miembros de su familia en el cuadro. Cuéntelos y nombre a cada uno. Utilice la frase de dos palabras MI + MIEMBRO DE LA FAMILIA.

There are _____ people in my family. Their names are _____.

Hay _____ personas en mi familia. Sus nombres son _____.

Session 3

Mealtime

La hora de comer

MEALTIME 3

Speech and Language Session Focus

Requests

Implementing language strategies during requests can be difficult for both parents and service providers. This interaction often goes something like this: the child wants something, we withhold the object until the child says a word, or two words, or makes a sign, and the child becomes upset. Meals can explode into tears, strategies are abandoned, and the confidence between parents and therapist can erode. Often the parent has employed this strategy independently or a professional or friend has suggested it. Although we can expect some frustration from the child when communication is being attempted, **negative emotion is the sign that we are working above a child's level.**

Mealtime provides us with a great opportunity to answer to a child's needs. For example, in the morning, invariably the child is hungry, thirsty, wet, or all of the above. He or she will need to make a request. Breakfast is an excellent time to practice requesting because it is routine, there are a small number of choices, the desire of the child is great, and it occurs daily.

Today's Plan

Use the mealtime routine to concretely identify how a child gets what he/she needs. A parent should be encouraged to:

- Offer smaller portions in an effort to increase requests. Food should not be withheld entirely.
- Put the food within the child's view, but at a distance.
- Give a choice of two items, one being the item the child desires.

Talk with the parent to see where the child is functioning, and then raise it one notch.

- If the child is reaching for a banana, have them point with a single finger.
- If a child makes sounds ("uh-uh") have her look at your lips as you say the name of the object before giving it to her.
- Practice the first sound of the word ("b" in banana).

Routines-Based Early Intervention Guidebook

MEALTIME 3.1

SIGN — Use signs and words together.
Water   **Drink**   **Eat**

MODEL — Use simple phrases.
"I want bananas"   **"Water, please"**

IMITATE — Imitate sounds, signs, words, and gestures that your child uses.
Imitate eating with a spoon.

LABEL — Name objects in your child's environment.
"Bowl"   **"Cereal"**

EXPAND — Add words to what your child says.
When your child says "Milk," you say, "More milk" or "Milk, please."

Practice these important words and add more of your own:

PLATE	JUICE
SPOON	APPLE
BOTTLE	BANANA
CUP	WANT
MILK	EAT

_____
_____
_____
_____
_____

MEALTIME

ACTIVITY IDEAS:
- Let your child help prepare a meal by gathering food items together. Talk about what you need and where things are (e.g., "up high," "inside the refrigerator").

- Have a picnic on the floor with pretend/toy foods. Have your child pretend to feed his/her favorite toy. Model requesting by signing/saying "more" and/or "I want _____."

- Cut out pictures of food and put them in groups (e.g., "I eat" and "I drink," or "sweet," "salty," "hot," "cold").

I will help my child by:

- _____
- _____

My child will:

_____
_____
_____
_____

THERAPIST SUGGESTS:

What happened?

-What did you do?
-What did your child say or do?
-What questions do you have?

_____
_____
_____
_____

La Hora de Comer

3.2

Señalar	Junte señas y palabras. **Agua** **Beber** **Comer**
Ofrecer **M**odelos	Diga frases sencillas. "**Quiero más**" "**Come manzana**"
Nombrar	Nombre objetos en su ambiente. "**Mesa**" "**Cuchara**"
Repetir	Repita sonidos, señas, palabras, y gestos que usa su niño/a. **Imite como su niño/a come con una cuchara.**
Ímitar	
Extender	Añada palabras a lo que dice su niño/a. **Si su niño/a diga "Leche,"** usted dígale, "**Más leche**" o "**Leche, por favor.**"

Practiquen estas palabras importantes y agreguen más:

PLATO	JUGO	_____
CUCHARA	MANZANA	_____
BOTELLA/TETA	BANANA	_____
TAZA	QUIERO	_____
LECHE	COMER	_____

La Hora de Comer

IDEAS DE ACTIVIDADES:
- Deje que su niño/a le ayude a preparar la comida buscando juntos los ingredientes. Indíquele lo que necesita y dónde está (por ejemplo, "arriba," "en la refri").

- Haga un picnic en el suelo con alimentos de juguete. Haga que su niño/a simule alimentar a su muñeco favorito. Muestrele a su niño/a como señalar/decir "más" y/o "Quiero _____."

- Recorte fotos de alimentos y póngalas en grupos (por ejemplo, "yo como" y "yo tomo," o "dulce," "salado," "caliente," "frío")

Ayudaré a mi niño/a así:

- _____
- _____

Mi niño/a va a:

_____
_____
_____
_____

> Sugerencia de la Terapista:

¿Qué pasó?
- ¿Qué hizo Ud.?
- ¿Qué dijo o hizo su niño/a?
- ¿Qué preguntas tiene Ud.?

_____
_____
_____

Routines-Based Early Intervention Guidebook

Mealtime/La Hora De Comer 3.3

Signs/Señas

Eat

Comer

Drink

Beber

Water

Agua

Mealtime/La Hora De Comer

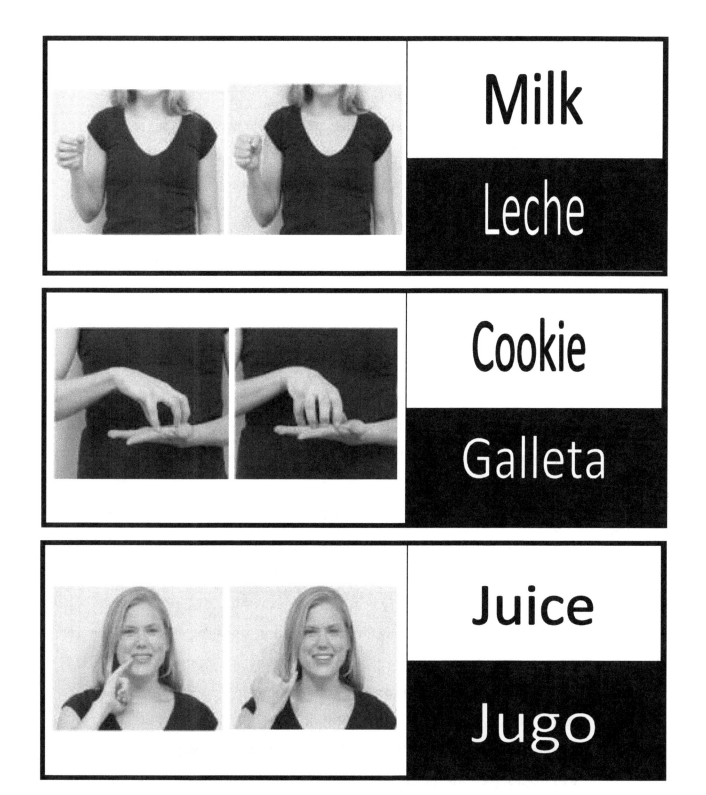

Teaching how to make requests 3.4

Children exhibit intentional communication from a very early age. It is not always verbal communication but it is intentional. Think about a one-year-old patting his mother's leg and putting his arms up to request to be picked up. While ultimately we want our children to request what they want and need verbally, we need to appreciate their use of non-verbal requests as well. They are communicating!

One thing you need to repeat over-and-over again until it is a truth for you is that the words that children hear drive the words they know and the words they use. If you want a child to make appropriate requests, he needs to see you doing it and needs to see children her age doing it also. The more children hear words, the sooner they internalize the words, understand the words, and use the words. So when your child is in their non-verbal requesting mode, give them the words they need to express their wants and needs. If they want to be picked up, you could say, "Up?" or "I want up."

Continuum of Making Requests

For many of us, the idea of non-verbal requests being the road to verbal requests is new. Let's take a look at a continuum of Requesting to Appropriate Verbal Requests. Our job is to identify where our child is functioning, try to get them to do more of that, and then work on the next level up.

1. **No requests**—not very common. Most prevalent in children with socio-pragmatic difficulties such as Autism Spectrum Disorder.
2. **Non-specific requests**— moving towards an area they want to go to. Observing an object or area with the eyes. Typical of babies exploring.
3. **Getting attention**—making eye contact, verbalizing, or calling attention to oneself. The reason the child is calling attention might not be apparent.
4. **Pulling an adult**—Intentional, physical, body motion in a direction. Can be accompanied by sounds, crying, or words.
5. **Pointing non-specifically**—Often used in negation, a child points in a direction away from something they do not want or something they want to get away from.

Teaching how to make requests

6. **Pointing at/touching an object**— Indicating the exact object or activity desired.
7. **Pulling an adult to an object**— Not only identifying what they want, but seeking assistance or interaction.
8. **Vocalizing to request**— Using a tone, cry, or sound intentionally to demonstrate that they want something.
9. **Approximating words**— Attempting to name the object and/or the person's name who can help them fulfill their request.
10. **Saying words**—Naming objects or people that the child wants to do something for them in their environment. E.g.., "Mommy!!"
11. **Combining verbalizations with gestures/signs**— Full commitment to get what he wants. Saying words, pulling an adult in a direction, pointing, and even crying.
12. **Static words + object or name or verb**—Using a learned word that is paired with an object to indicate a desire such as: more, please, yes, or no
13. **Making a request**— Wow! Did you know how much development goes into getting what we want? By understanding this continuum of development, we can identify the level at which our little ones are functioning and help them move in a the direction of making a request.

Helping Children to Make Requests

Helping a child learn how to make requests requires identifying situations where a child really wants something and showing them how to request it. We can create situations or we can rely on natural situations when a child is already asking for something. Two quick notes:

1. **Do not restrict food**— We don't want to turn an eating situation into a battle. Meal time is a great time to help them request but we want to immediately reward any attempt and not make the situation frustrating.
2. **Immediately reward success**— The teaching of a request should take just a few seconds. Once they comply, celebrate and move on so that request making is not linked to frustration.

Teaching how to make requests 3.4

Requesting is a natural experience that happens all day long. Kids are heavily dependent on adults which makes it even more frustrating when a child is struggling to communicate their wants and needs. Here are a couple tips for children who are struggling in this area and ways to find opportunities to support request making throughout the day.

Tips for Highly Unintelligible Children

1. **Use visual cues for frequently requested items.** Children will have an easier time making a request if they can see pictures of the objects or locations. Teachers can keep pictures in their classroom of all of the locations in school such as the playground or centers. Parents can have pictures on their phone or tablet that a child can scroll through to choose from.
2. **Give the child a choice of two objects if you do not understand her.** Sometimes a child will point in the direction of an entire wall of toys and get frustrated when we don't know what they want. Show the child two objects and have them make a choice between this reduced number.
3. **Acknowledge the communication attempt.** Children grow increasingly frustrated if they don't get what they want and know that they are not understood. Begin by saying: "I see you are telling me you want something, is that correct? What is it?"
4. **Separate the communication attempt from saying "No."** We can't give children everything they want. However, children who struggle making requests feel like they *never* get what they want. We need to acknowledge that we understood them, tell them why they can't have it, and/or when they will be able to have it.

The Best Opportunities for Making Requests

1. Moving between locations: "Do you want to go to the park, pool, library...?"
2. Choosing between activities: "Do you want to read a book or write?"
3. Choosing within activities: "It's art time, do you want to paint, draw, color?"
4. Giving them two choices when you want both outcomes: Do you want to clean up or do homework first?"
5. Choosing between foods: "Do you want to eat X or Y today?"

Making Requests Activity

Mealtime/La hora de comer

Help your child learn how to make requests. Cut off labels from his/her favorite foods. Help your child point to a food or say the word. Add the words "more" or "please" if your child is using many words.

Ayude a su niño/a en aprender como pedir cosas. Corte la etiqueta de su comida favorita. Ayúdele en apuntar o decir la palabra. Añada las palabras "más" o "por favor" si su niño/a puede usar muchas palabras.

Thinking about communication/Pensando en la comunicación

How does your child let you know he/she is hungry? ¿Cómo sabe que su niño/a tiene hambre?	How can you add signs or words? ¿Cómo puede usar más señas o palabras?
How does he/she ask for more food ¿Cómo pide más comida?	How can you add signs or words? ¿Cómo puede usar más señas o palabras?
What food words does he/she say? ¿Qué palabras de comida dice?	What other words can you practice? ¿Qué otras palabras puede practicar?

Session 4

Getting Dressed

Vestirse

Getting Dressed 4

Speech and Language Session Focus

Expanding Phrases Activities— Cloze Techniques

Cloze techniques involve giving a child the first part of a sentence (e.g., "Put on your ____"), in an attempt to encourage the child to produce the missing word (e.g., "pants"). Often, parents may watch a service provider use this technique successfully, but then have less success on their own. What parents may not have picked up on is the structure that has been created in order to elicit a specific word. Cloze techniques are not merely fill-in-the-blanks, but are the process of guiding a child to a successful response. This is achieved by creating a routine that has an order and happens frequently.

Getting dressed provides a routine that happens frequently and employs the same objects. A child knows which piece of clothing is next because he or she has learned the routine or because his or her parent is holding it.

Today's Plan

Parents should be encouraged to use open-ended sentences that their child can complete to teach new vocabulary. When the child is successful with this technique, the parent should try to use it in other daily activities.

- Begin with a fixed expression and hold up the object. For example, while holding a pair of socks, say to the child, "Here are your _____," and wait for your child to respond. If he/she doesn't respond, fill in the blank for them. "Here are your socks!"
- Add sequencing words. For example, while holding socks and shoes, say "First put on your _____," and wait for a response. If correct, say, "Next, put on your _____," and wait for a response.
- Add questions. For example, "What else? Your _____," and wait for a response.
- Joke with the child by calling an object by the wrong name and see if he/she names it correctly.

Getting Dressed

4.1

Sign	Use signs and words together. **Pants** **Shirt** **Shoes**
Model	Use simple phrases. **"Sock on"** **"Put on pants"**
Imitate	Imitate sounds, signs, words, and gestures that your child uses. **Imitate getting dressed.**
Label	Name objects in your child's environment. **"Shoe" "Leg"**
Expand	Add words to what your child says. **When your child says "Shirt," you say, "Shirt on."**

Practice these important words and add more of your own:

WEAR	TAKE OFF	_____
SHIRT	HAT	_____
PANTS	SOCKS	_____
DRESS	DIAPER	_____
SHOES	UNDERWEAR	_____

GETTING DRESSED

ACTIVITY IDEAS:

- Gather a variety of clothing items (e.g., pants, shirts, socks, hats) and play dress-up with your child. Take turns "putting on" the clothing.

- Have your child help you put away the laundry. Practice labeling each item of clothing as you put it away.

- Read the book *Froggy Gets Dressed* by Jonathan London and talk about the clothes you need when you go outside.

I will help my child by:

- _____
- _____

My child will:

_____
_____
_____
_____

THERAPIST SUGGESTS:

What happened?

-What did you do?
-What did your child say or do?
-What questions do you have?

_____
_____
_____
_____

Vestirse   4.2

Señalar	Junte señas y palabras. **Pantalones Camisa Zapatos**
Ofrecer **M**odelos	Diga frases sencillas. **"Dos zapatos" "Pon calcetines"**
Nombrar	Nombre objetos en su ambiente. **"Zapato" "Pierna"**
Repetir **Í**mitar	Repita sonidos, señas, palabras, y gestos que usa su niño/a. **Imite como su niño/a se pone la ropa cuando se viste.**
Extender	Añada palabras a lo que dice su niño/a. **Cuando su niño/a diga "Camisa," usted dígale, "Pon camisa."**

Practiquen estas palabras importantes y agreguen más:

ME PONGO	ME QUITO	_____
CAMISA	GORRA	_____
PANTALONES	CALCETINES	_____
VESTIDO	PAÑAL	_____
ZAPATOS	CALZONCILLOS	_____

VESTIRSE

IDEAS DE ACTIVIDADES:
- Reúna varias prendas de vestir (por ejemplo, pantalones, camisas, calcetines, sombreros) y juegue a disfrazarse con su niño/a. Tomen turnos para ponerse la ropa.

- Pídale a su niño/a que le ayude a guardar la ropa lavada. Practique dándole nombre a cada pieza de ropa mientras la guarda.

- Léale el libro *Froggy Se Viste* de Jonathan London y hablen de la ropa que se necesita para salir.

Ayudaré a mi niño/a así:

- _____
- _____

Mi niño/a va a:

_____
_____
_____
_____

SUGERENCIA DE LA TERAPISTA:

¿Qué pasó?

- ¿Qué hizo Ud.?
- ¿Qué dijo o hizo su niño/a?
- ¿Qué preguntas tiene Ud.?

_____
_____
_____

Getting Dressed/Vestirse 4.3

Signs/Señas

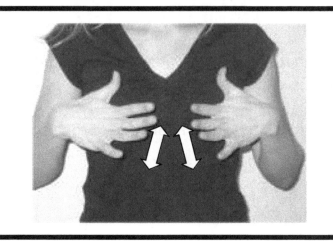
Get dressed / Vestirse

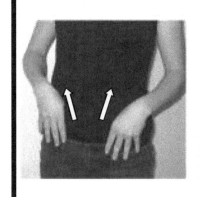 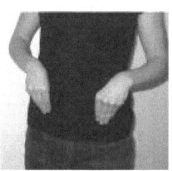
Pants / Pantalones

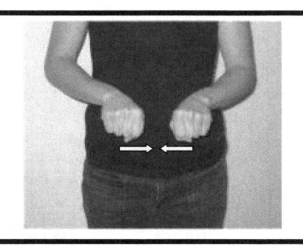
Shoes / Zapatos

Getting Dressed/Vestirse

Shirt

Camisa

Hat

Gorra

Diaper

Pañal

TEACHING EXPANDED PHRASES   4.4

Some children are highly verbal in certain situations and really struggle to communicate in others. As an example, many children engage in personal interactions well but then when it comes time to demonstrate any sort of knowledge or academic ability, they are left with very little to say. Cloze procedures are a support we can provide to children to help them be successful with structures that are more complex than they are able to produce on their own.

In a cloze procedure, we provide the portion of the structure that the child cannot produce and allow them to complete the part of the structure they are able to produce. For example, a child is requesting a toy car. The parent says, "I want…," leaving the word "want" hanging in the air and then the child fills in with "car." Or the teachers says: "The train goes…" and the child says, "Choo choo."

Strategies to Expand a Child's Utterance

Successful utterance expansion depends on having a child identify the basic parts of a phrase and then add to it. This can easily be accomplished with visual or auditory support.

Sentence Strips

Think of the words of a sentence as a series of blocks. Even with children who are not yet reading, we can point to the words in a sentence every time we say a word. This provides visual representation for each thing being said. At the school level, words can be written on different cards and physically assembled. Either way, we are dividing the big utterance into its components so the child can see it getting bigger or smaller.

Auditory and Tactile Techniques

Clapping along with a sentence, tapping on the body, or even stomping our feet with each word gives a child multiple sensory cues about the different parts of a phase. A child can clap with you three times and then repeat and clap with you, "I want milk." The auditory and tactile input the child gets from clapping helps her successfully produce a three-word phrase.

Flip-boards

Flip boards are visual versions of Cloze procedures. As an example, on the board it says, "I want," and then the child can flip through a series of pictures to finish the phase.

Teaching Expanded Phrases

These boards are easily transferable to different daily routines by maintaining the board and swapping out the options.

Use Categories Instead of Object Names

Objects are naturally grouped. We have toys, clothes, foods, and everything that naturally goes within the group. For children who are really struggling, it is often better to teach a more general word so that the child has multiple opportunities to practice the word throughout the day. For example, the child can say, "I want food," rather than having to choose between the multitude of food objects.

Use Verbs Instead of Object Names

Another way to reduce the vocabulary for struggling children but still expand their phrases is to use verbs. Rather than naming all the toys or all the foods, they can just learn "I want (to) eat" or "I want (to) play." These verbs encompass all of the objects that would be used to carry out the activity. While this is not where we want the child to be eventually, it is a great small step to get the child to make general requests and build specificity later.

Expanding Phrases in the Real World

Parents need to know that there are dozens of opportunities to expand a child's utterance each day. Often, they need examples. Here are a few:

1. The Store – Children point out an infinite number of objects while shopping. It is a great opportunity to add numbers, adjectives, and names to anything they see and say. For example, cookie can become want/good/yellow/one/my/big/chocolate cookie.

2. Commuting—Children see an infinite number of objects passing through the window while you drive. You can help them better describe everything that is in their world or use the radio to sing their favorite song with them.

Expanding Phrases Activity 4.4

Getting Dressed/Vestirse

Color the clothes and draw a line to where it goes on the body. Use cloze procedures to describe where the clothes go. "Socks go on your…"

Coloree la ropa y trace una línea a la parte del cuerpo en donde se pone esa ropa. Utilice los procedimientos decCloze para describir donde se va la ropa. "Los calcetines van en su …"

Session 5

Toys and Playtime

Jugando

TOYS AND PLAYTIME 5

SPEECH AND LANGUAGE SESSION FOCUS

TURN-TAKING

The idea that communication is the process of taking turns may be more obvious to service providers than it is to parents. Parents with typical language skills may never have compared speech to throwing balls or tennis matches. A discussion about joint turn-taking is an excellent way to compliment a mother and father on their parenting abilities. Turn-taking inherently makes sense and usually already exists in communicative attempts and games like ball rolling. Parents should be encouraged to use turn-taking in other play activities as well and incorporate simple language, such as, "My turn" and "Your turn."

What we as interventionists know is that using a ball encourages joint turn-taking because the activity is *controlled* by having a single element (i.e., the ball). The activity will stop unless someone takes a turn. Other play activities should likewise be controlled by the parent. For example, in playing blocks, all blocks can be in a bucket and each person can only take one out at a time. While dressing a doll, all clothes can be hidden and each person can choose one piece of clothing at a time. Snacks, such as raisins, can be set on the table one at a time and each person takes one when it is his or her turn. Turn-taking is elementary but it is not so simple that it should be overlooked. A parent who can successfully mediate control of joint turn-taking can successfully encourage communication.

TODAY'S PLAN

Discuss turn-taking and identify where it is already taking place throughout the day (e.g., greetings, play, games). Encourage fun turn-taking activities that:

- Include one object or gesture.
- Do not last long or become boring.
- Include a third or fourth older person when possible.

Toys and Playtime

SIGN	Use signs and words together. **My turn** **Play** **Ball**
MODEL	Use simple phrases. **"Throw ball" "More blocks here"**
IMITATE	Imitate sounds, signs, words, and gestures that your child uses. **Imitate car and animal noises.**
LABEL	Name objects in your child's environment. **"Bear" "Ball"**
EXPAND	Add words to what your child says. **When your child says "Truck," you say, "Go truck."**

Practice these important words and add more of your own:

CAR	TRAIN	_____
TRUCK	PAPER	_____
BAT	CRAYONS	_____
PUZZLE	BOOK	_____
BLOCKS	DOLL	_____

Toys and Playtime

ACTIVITY IDEAS:
- Throw or roll a ball back and forth with your child. Say/sign "I want the ball" or "My turn" to model taking turns for your child.

- Put toys out of reach and have your child request them by saying/signing the name of the toy or "I want _____."

- Name each item as you clean up the toys and use the same phrase each time (e.g., "Put away block," "Put away ball.")

I will help my child by:

- _____
- _____

My child will:

_____
_____
_____
_____

Therapist Suggests:

What happened?

-What did you do?
-What did your child say or do?
-What questions do you have?

_____
_____
_____
_____

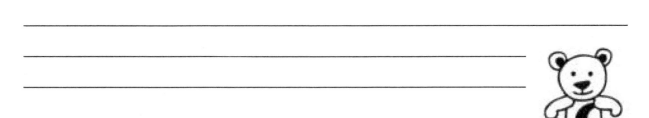

JUGANDO 5.2

Señalar	Junte señas y palabras. **Mi turno Jugar Pelota**
Ofrecer **M**odelos	Diga frases sencillas. **"Tira la pelota" "Más bloques"**
Nombrar	Nombre objetos en su ambiente. **"Oso" "Pelota"**
Repetir **Í**mitar	Repita sonidos, señas, palabras, y gestos que usa su niño/a. **Imite sonidos de animales y carros.**
Extender	Añada palabras a lo que dice su niño/a. **Cuando su niño/a diga "Carro," usted dígale, "El carro va."**

Practiquen estas palabras importantes y agreguen más:

CARRO	TREN	_____
CAMIÓN	PAPEL	_____
BATE	COLORES	_____
ROMPECABEZAS	LIBRO	_____
BLOQUES	MUÑECA	_____

JUGANDO

IDEAS DE ACTIVIDADES:
- Tírele o ponga a rodar una pelota de un lado a otro con su niño/a. Dígale con palabras o señas "Quiero la pelota" o "Mi turno" para que le modele como tomar su turno.

- Coloque los juguetes fuera del alcance de su niño/a y haga que los pida diciendo el nombre del juguete, mediante señas o "Quiero _____."

- Nombre cada juguete cuando los recoja y use la misma frase cada vez (por ejemplo, "Guarda los bloques," "Guarda la pelota").

Ayudaré a mi niño/a así:

- _____
- _____

Mi niño/a va a:

_____
_____
_____

SUGERENCIA DE LA TERAPISTA:

¿Qué pasó?
- ¿Qué hizo Ud.?
- ¿Qué dijo o hizo su niño/a?
- ¿Qué preguntas tiene Ud.?

_____
_____
_____
_____

Toys and Playtime/Jugando

Signs/Señas

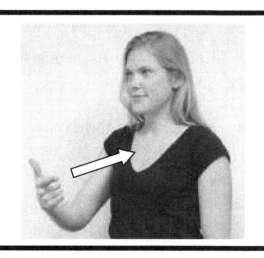 **My turn** / Mi turno

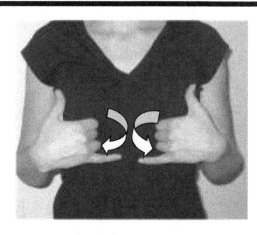 **Play** / Jugar

 **Fell down** / Se cayó

Toys and Playtime/Jugando

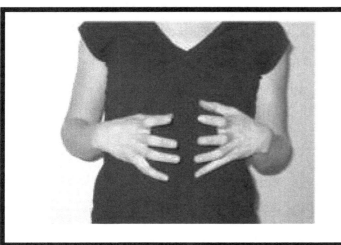

Ball

Pelota

Blocks

Bloques

Baby

Bebé

Routines-Based Early Intervention Guidebook

Teaching how to Take Turns   5.4

Turn-taking skills are a building block of communication. In order to take turns in communicative exchanges, young children first must learn how to take turns physically through activities, games and play. For children who really struggle with taking turns, we often work on turn-taking skills at a non-verbal level to build this foundational skill.

This might be as simple as rolling a ball back and forth. On the surface, this many not seem like it is supporting communication but it is actually helping to build this important foundational skill.

Special Note: It is important to create opportunities for the child to lead and participate as an equal partner. Too often, an adult initiates and the child plays the roll of responder when it is his or her turn. Stronger turn-taking skills can be built if the child is also taught how to initiate and how to lead others while taking turns. Here are some great examples of turn-taking activities.

Powerful Turn-taking Play Activities

1. **Game playing** - All games require turns. This is sometimes difficult to learn even for the most developed child. The best games require turns for the game to continue. For example, putting a puzzle together when each child holds the next piece. When working in groups, choose games that have rapid transitions between players. Long intervals can introduce behaviors that don't allow the child to learn turn-taking.

2. **Playing with your voice**— Children love to hear different voices and make and imitate sounds. You can imitate a cartoon character, speak with a stuffed animal, change the speed and volume of your voice, or sing rather than speak. Children are prone to take a turn and imitate you.

3. **Cumulative play**—Activities such as puzzles, building a tower with blocks or assembling a racetrack require all of the members to take turns. As an adult, you can control the activity by handing out the pieces one-by-one so that everyone sees who is next and waits. Cumulative games are really satisfying because there is

TEACHING HOW TO TAKE TURNS

always a successful and obvious completion.

4. **Simon Says**—Simon Says places the power to tell someone else to do something in the hands of a child. This is a great reciprocal activity because turn-taking is a two way street and children shouldn't always be the follower. Any chance we get to put them in charge will motivate them to understand how to take turns.

5. **Nursery rhymes and poems**— Reciting nursery rhymes or song activities where a child acts out a sequence of events creates a memorizable sequence of turns. This is another example of a way to take turns without having the adult always be guiding as the child follows. For example, younger students can produce the hand movements of Itzy Bitzy Spider in order for the adult to keep singing or vice versa. For older students, complex group clapping and singing sequences have to be memorized by two individuals who take turns to make the rhyme work.

Turn-taking Activities in the Classroom

Turn-taking eventually evolves into the conversational abilities of older students and adults. It assists emotional development as we listen to other's problems and share our own. We learn to participate through taking turns without feeling excluded. Eventually, we learn to participate in activities that we may not want to for the chance to do something that we prefer. This all begins with activities focusing on taking turns.

1. **Raising your hand**—Why are some students able to participate by raising their hands while others are not? Anxiety can undermine a child's ability to take turns. This comes in the form of competing to respond and blurting out an answer. Or, the opposite can occur and anxiety can drive children into silence even when they know the right answer. The use of visual cues and physical objects can bring either of these children back towards the center. Children who over-respond can be given a daily chart allowing them a set number of responses and praise when they allow others to respond. A physical object such a stuff animal can be employed during carpet time by passing it to the one child who has the turn to talk.

2. **Timers and Centers**—Sometimes it can feel like infinity to a child who wants to speak or participate in an activity. A timer can be used to allow them to know

Teaching how to Take Turns 5.4

when it is their turn. There are apps with visual timers to allow children to actually see how much time is left. This is especially effective during centers if a class is expected to rotate between activities. Children learn best from other children so if an entire group is moving in a direction, it is easier to join the fun.

FIRST	THEN

3. **FIRST-THEN Systems**— FIRST-THEN systems are powerful for changing moods and are especially helpful for children who have behavioral or emotional components in their educational plan. When a child is having difficulty waiting to take her turn, she can be told "First X, then Y." This system is really successful because a single system can be used throughout the day. Often parents and teachers will use a small whiteboard that is divided in half and with the words FIRST and THEN written at the top. Pictures or words can be added and taken away rapidly and give the child a sense of security because they know their requests have been heard and are coming after the first activity is finished.

4. **Line Leader**—Line leader is actually a pretty sophisticated turn taking routine. A child often has to wait half a month to participate as line leader. These routines often offer multiple jobs such as door opener or the caboose. When a child has to wait across multiple days for something they need to do, it is best to show a visual progression of everyone involved moving closer toward their turn.

5. **Helping**—The home and classroom offer a multitude of multi-step activities that teach complex turn-taking. The best of these activities allow several different children to hold objects to participate in a routine. Cooking for example, requires multiple ingredients to be put into the recipe in a specific order. Another example is assembling objects for an activity. At home this could mean setting the table. At lunch this could be gathering the toys for the playground or the nametags for lunch. Any activity for helping requires a series of steps and therefore creates a natural environment for taking turns.

Turn-Taking Activity

Toys and Playtime/Jugando

Take turns counting and coloring these toys. Draw a line to the correct number below.

Tome turnos contando y coloreando estos juguetes. Dibuje una línea al número correcto abajo.

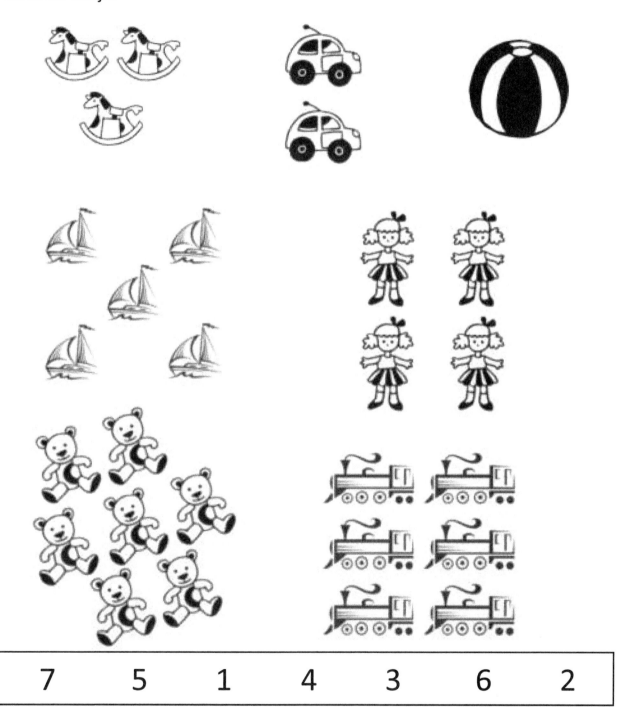

| 7 | 5 | 1 | 4 | 3 | 6 | 2 |

Session 6

Outside

Afuera

Outside

Speech and Language Session Focus

Change of State - Identifying Emotions

As interventionists, we know how to describe something that is constant or non-changing (e.g., the block is red, it is big), and how to describe something that changes (e.g., the soup is hot). Individual service plans often focus on the non-changing attributes. However, descriptions of changing states should not be ignored.

Recognizing changes of state creates the groundwork for understanding our internal emotions and how we interact with others. Socially, a child understands not to hit someone because he or she knows how it feels to be hit. A child will learn to share because he or she knows how it feels to have something shared with him or her. The weather, time of day, and seasons provide opportunities to observe the fluid changes in our environment.

Today's Plan

Parents should be encouraged to point out the obvious (e.g., "It is hot out here today!"). They should also identify an emotion that a child is feeling and commiserate with them. For example, "I see that you feel sad that you can't play with the ball. I feel sad for you too. Tomorrow we can practice being more careful so that it doesn't go in the street, and I won't have to put it away." Identify changes of state in:

- Food temperature
- The sun rising or setting
- The weather
- The child's emotions
- The parents' emotions

OUTSIDE

6.1

SIGN	Use signs and words together. **Jump Swing Bird**
MODEL	Use simple phrases. **"Play outside" "Go to park"**
IMITATE	Imitate sounds, signs, words, and gestures that your child uses. **Imitate digging and building.**
LABEL	Name objects in your child's environment. **"Sign" "Tree"**
EXPAND	Add words to what your child says. **When your child says "Car," you say, "Blue car."**

Practice these important words and add more of your own:

PARK	LEAVES	_____
TOYS	YARD	_____
BICYCLE	TREE	_____
BALL	BIRD	_____
PLAY	DOG	_____

OUTSIDE

ACTIVITY IDEAS:
- Label things you see when you go for a walk (e.g., trees, leaves, flowers). Talk about their colors (e.g., sky - blue, leaves - green)

- Imitate environmental noises that you hear: "beep beep," "woof woof," etc.

- Play with different types of movements (e.g., walking, running, jumping) and talk about them using opposites: slow/fast, up/down, inside/outside, stop/go.

I will help my child by:

- _____
- _____

My child will:

_____
_____
_____

THERAPIST SUGGESTS:

What happened?

-What did you do?
-What did your child say or do?
-What questions do you have?

_____
_____
_____

Afuera

6.2

Señalar	Junte señas y palabras. **Brincar Columpio Pájaro**
Ofrecer **M**odelos	Diga frases sencillas. **"Juguemos afuera" "Vamos al parque"**
Nombrar	Nombre objetos en su ambiente. **"Letrero" "Árbol"**
Repetir **Í**mitar	Repita sonidos, señas, palabras, y gestos que usa su niño/a. **Imite a su niño/a cuando esté jugando y construyendo cosas.**
Extender	Añada palabras a lo que dice su niño/a. **Cuando su niño/a diga "Carro," usted dígale, "Carro azul."**

Practiquen estas palabras importantes y agreguen más:

PARQUE	HOJAS	_____
JUGUETES	JARDÍN	_____
BICICLETA	ÁRBOL	_____
PELOTA	PÁJARO	_____
JUGAR	PERRO	_____

AFUERA

IDEAS DE ACTIVIDADES:
- Dele nombre a las cosas que ven cuando van de paseo (por ejemplo, árboles, hojas, flores). Hable de sus colores (por ejemplo, cielo - azul, hojas - verdes)

- Imite los ruidos ambientales que se escuchen: "bip bip," "guau guau," etc.

- Juegue con diferentes tipos de movimientos (por ejemplo, caminar, correr, saltar) y hable de ellos utilizando los opuestos: lento/rápido, arriba/abajo, adentro/afuera, parar/seguir.

Ayudaré a mi niño/a así:

- _____
- _____

Mi niño/a va a:

_____
_____
_____
_____

> SUGERENCIA DE LA TERAPISTA:

¿Qué pasó?

- ¿Qué hizo Ud.?
- ¿Qué dijo o hizo su niño/a?
- ¿Qué preguntas tiene Ud.?

_____
_____
_____

Outside/Afuera

6.3

Signs/Señas

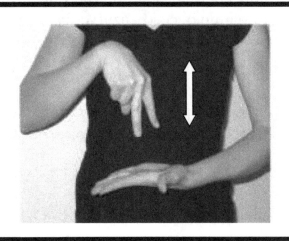	**Jump** / Brincar
	**Swing** / Columpio
 	**Tree** / Árbol

OUTSIDE/AFUERA

TEACHING HOW TO IDENTIFY EMOTIONS 6.4

An emotion is the expression of a person's inner feeling. When this inner feeling grows, it manifests itself in an outer expression which we interpret as being positive, neutral, or negative. Some of the first emotions that children express are joy, fear, and anger. Around 30-months-old, children start to express emotions that relate to the way they see themselves such as embarrassment, guilt, or pride. As a child grows up, we teach them how to express emotions in a healthy way and how to change if we are experiencing an emotion that is not desirable. They learn how to talk about their emotions, how to regulate their feelings, as well as how to show their emotions in appropriate ways.

Well-developed children are said to have "emotional competence." This means that a child can identify what he is feeling, what other people are feeling, and can modify emotions to better deal with certain situations. Children with emotional competence are likely to do well in school and engage in positive relationships with other children and family members.

Children with emotional competence are more likely to be empathetic and can understand how others might be feeling. They are also more likely to help others and to find ways to deal with negative situations. Children who have had negative experiences early in their life may have trouble dealing with emotions. This is where we come in. We teach the appropriate responses in safe situations so that a child can generalize the ability to times they need it the most. Here are three quick tips:

1. **Do not practice in the middle of a "meltdown."** Use calm times for learning and to practice new strategies.

2. **Use words that a child can understand.** Even with older children who have emotional issues, they may only be able to identify with 3-5 core emotions. Choose words that make since with them at the beginning and expand into more complex words over time. For instance, "mad" is good enough for describing emotions like angry, frustrated, upset, and furious.

3. **Use real-life examples.** Those meltdowns or blowups that we are all so afraid of and trying to avoid are now your perfect teaching opportunity. No, it is not something that we want to experience. But, if we sit in that episode and work to employ the following strategies, we begin to learn, teach, and make progress.

Teaching how to identify emotions

Children experience many of the same emotions that we as adults do. However, it is their response to the emotion that we deem inappropriate and work to change. Here are some strategies to help a child to express emotions appropriately.

1. **Assign Feelings to Colors** – Teach children the broad spectrum of available emotions. For younger children, assign emotions to colors first (red, yellow, blue, green) and have the child identify with a color. "I am mad, I feel red today." More complex words (frustrated) can be added to the same colors for older children.

2. **Name the Feeling** – Help your children understand their emotions by first giving the feelings names. For example, you could say, "You didn't get the top you wanted, you are sad." By naming the emotion that the child is feeling, you are helping the child to develop a vocabulary of emotions.

3. **Identify Emotions in Others** – By using cartoons, images, and other children, we can help a child identify the emotional state of someone without concern for one feeling defensive. It also shows that experiencing emotions is a natural process that we all go through.

4. **Vary the Response to an Event** – Choose a single event and discuss the many outcomes that can occur. For example, if a child in a classroom is upset and is taking a break, a group discussion could occur. "Jenny is crying because her crayon broke. What are some things she could do when her crayon breaks other than crying?"

5. **Use Mirrors** – We have all heard the response when we ask a child if he is mad: "I am not mad!" Using mirrors to imitate emotions when a child is content helps them identify the facial features associated with a feeling. This way, when they are experiencing an emotion they have a way to check in with themselves and use their body to help them identify how they are feeling. For example, when we are mad we are hot, sweaty, tense, frowning, etc.

6. **Teach Feeling Words** – Once it is established that a child knows that there are different emotional options, it is time to start introducing her to the wealth of emotions that we get to experience every day. These words are great for a word

TEACHING HOW TO IDENTIFY EMOTIONS 6.4

wall in school. If you are using the color spectrum idea, add them to the appropriate color.

Uncomfortable	Lonely	Angry	Overwhelmed
Stubborn	Interested	Worried	Shy
Fantastic	Embarrassed	Ignored	Peaceful
Relieved	Loving	Silly	Friendly
Jealous	Generous	Impatient	Calm
Excited	Safe	Tense	Important
Confused	Proud	Disappointed	Frustrated
Brave	Cheerful	Surprised	Curious

7. **Share Your Own State** – Children learn best from mimicry. We should take the opportunity to share an event and identify an emotion that is attached to it. "I had a difficult day at work. I am flustered." "It makes me feel bad when John kicks me and that is why he had to go to the principal's office."

8. **Engage Physically with a Child** – Emotions change rapidly when contact is made with the child. Give hugs, high fives, fist bumps, or pats on the back. Human contact shows caring and empathy and can aid in diffusing a situation.

9. **Sing Songs** – Songs are fun and naturally cause the body to resonate with emotion. Use songs as a way to teach this skill. There are many songs available such as "If You are Happy and You Know It." Otherwise you can make up your own or put on their favorite song to experience an emotional change.

10. **Draw Emotions** - All children know the difference between a happy and sad smiley face. Draw the face and have the child draw a smile, straight mouth, or frown to express themselves. Older children can draw the event that is causing the negative emotion.

Giving children a variety of ways to identify their emotions and express how they are feeling is a critical piece to emotional development. Having a good way to express emotions can reduce frustration in children, thereby reducing undesired behaviors.

Identifying Emotions Activity
Outside/Afuera

Draw a line from each object to the place where you would find it. Talk to your child about what makes them happy when they are inside and what makes them happy when they are outside.

Dibuje una línea desde cada objeto hasta el lugar en donde lo encontraría. Hable con su hijo sobre lo que los hace felices cuando están dentro y lo que los hace felices cuando están afuera.

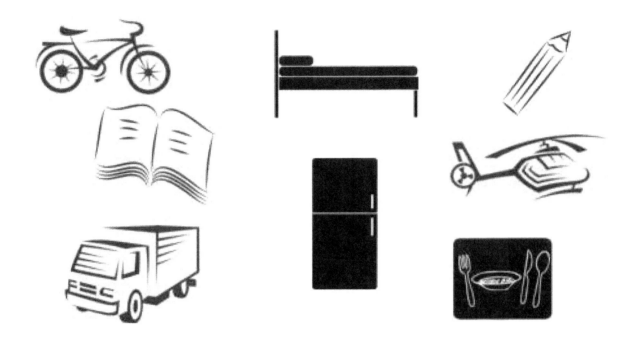

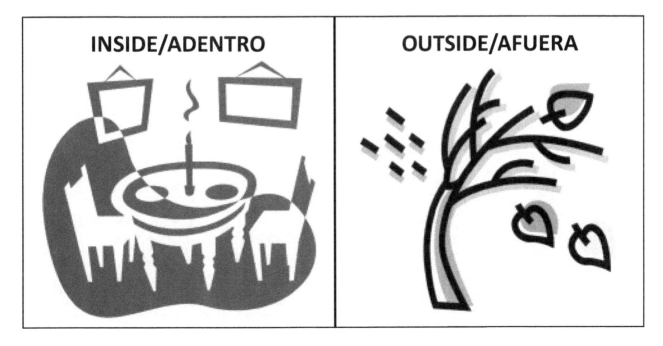

Session 7

In the Car

En el carro

IN THE CAR

SPEECH AND LANGUAGE SESSION FOCUS

DESCRIBING

In order to provide the best opportunity to describe an object or event, a comparison needs to be made. Intuitively, interventionists choose a group of like objects (e.g., blocks) and help a child to identify what may be different (e.g., color, size). Driving in a car presents many natural opportunities to practice this skill.

A simple errand or trip across town provides views of similar objects that are constantly changing. Passengers are surrounded by vehicles, buildings, trees, and signs. These objects vary by size and color as the car changes locations. Encourage the caregivers to choose one group (e.g., cars) as we do in the clinical setting and highlight differences (e.g., big car, blue car). Objects can be described in several forms such as, comments (e.g., "Look at the..."), observations (e.g., "That ... is big!), or by playing games (e.g., "I spy with my little eye...").

TODAY'S PLAN

Explain how driving time can be used to describe objects.
Parents should be encouraged to:

- Identify groups of like objects that the child can compare (e.g., cars, blocks).
- Describe the colors and sizes of cars on the road.
- Choose an object (e.g., trees) and describe it in many different ways.

IN THE CAR   7.1

SIGN	Use signs and words together. **Car** **Stop** **Let's go**
MODEL	Use simple phrases. **"Big bus"** **"I see a train"**
IMITATE	Imitate sounds, signs, words, and gestures that your child uses. **Imitate vehicle noises.**
LABEL	Name objects in your child's environment. **"Car"** **"Radio"**
EXPAND	Add words to what your child says. **When your child says "Train," you say, "Look, a train."**

Practice these important words and add more of your own:

CAR	BOAT	_____
BUS	TRAIN	_____
STREET	STORE	_____
FAST	LET'S GO	_____
RED	BLUE	_____

In the Car

ACTIVITY IDEAS:
- Describe vehicles you see using descriptive words (e.g., big truck, red bike, fast car, loud horn).

- Model using complete sentences to help your child tell you what they see while riding in the car (e.g., "I see a big truck," "I see a cow").

- Sing the "Wheels on the Bus" song and encourage imitation of actions and words.

I will help my child by:

- _____
- _____

My child will:

_____
_____
_____

THERAPIST SUGGESTS:

What happened?

    -What did you do?
    -What did your child say or do?
    -What questions do you have?

_____
_____
_____

En el Carro

7.2

SEÑALAR	Junte señas y palabras. **Carro Parar Vámonos**
OFRECER **M**ODELOS	Diga frases sencillas. **"Carro grande" "Veo un tren"**
NOMBRAR	Nombre objetos en su ambiente. **"Carro" "Radio"**
REPETIR **Í**MITAR	Repita sonidos, señas, palabras, y gestos que usa su niño/a. **Imite los carros, su bocina, o canciones.**
EXTENDER	Añada palabras a lo que dice su niño/a. **Cuando su niño/a diga "Tren," usted dígale, "Mira, un tren."**

Practiquen estas palabras importantes y agreguen más:

CARRO	BARCO	_____
AUTOBÚS	TREN	_____
CALLE	TIENDA	_____
RÁPIDO	VÁMONOS	_____
ROJO	AZUL	_____

En el Carro

IDEAS DE ACTIVIDADES:

- Describa los vehículos que ven, usando calificativos (por ejemplo, camión grande, bicicleta roja, carro rápido, bocina fuerte).

- Modele hablando con oraciones completas para ayudar a su niño/a a que le cuente lo que ve mientras van en el carro (por ejemplo, "Veo un camión grande," "Veo a una vaca").

- Cante la canción "Las Ruedas del Autobús" y estimule la imitación de acciones y palabras.

Ayudaré a mi niño/a así:

- _____
- _____

Mi niño/a va a:

_____
_____
_____

> SUGERENCIA DE LA TERAPISTA:

¿Qué pasó?

- ¿Qué hizo Ud.?
- ¿Qué dijo o hizo su niño/a?
- ¿Qué preguntas tiene Ud.?

_____
_____
_____

In the Car/En el Carro

Signs/Señas

In the Car/En el Carro

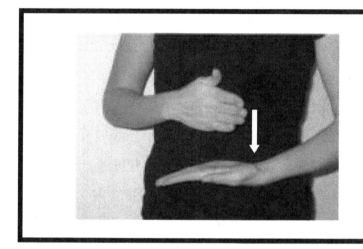	**Stop** **Parar**
 	**Come** **Venir**
 	**Let's go** **Vámonos**

Routines-Based Early Intervention Guidebook

Teaching How to Describe 7.4

Too often, when we are working to increase a child's expressive language, the conversation centers around vocabulary. Vocabulary building is a huge focus for young children at home, at developmental centers, and in the schools. Lessons are taught, tests are taken, and a child's progress is based on what they can remember, name, spell, and write. However, some children do not acquire vocabulary at the same rate as the majority of their peers. Attempts to teach more vocabulary are usually not successful because the focus is put on the word count or word lists rather than improving the process in which the vocabulary is acquired in the first place.

We can dramatically improve how children are communicating by shifting the focus from the quantity of words they use to the quality of what they say. We can do this successfully by improving how a child describes. At its core, describing is the ability to accurately use adjectives, as well as quantitative and qualitative concepts to increase our knowledge about an object. There is an added bonus to working on how a child describes. Rather than teaching lists of vocabulary that may not be used again, we are teaching words that can be applied to any new concept that we encounter. Let's begin with the general descriptive categories and then share ways to improve the way a child describes at home and at school.

Descriptions:	**Cookie**	**Senses**	**Use Verbs**	
Number	1 cookie		Eat	Eat cookies
Size	big cookie	Sight	Bake	Bake cookies
Color	brown cookie	Taste	Want	I want cookies
Type	chocolate cookie	Touch		
Opinion	I love cookies	Hear		
Experience	I ate a cookie once	Smell		

Teaching How to Describe

You can see by this list that we are building knowledge about cookies so that remembering and using the word "cookie" becomes possible for the student. We cannot provide every student with experiences of all the places and objects on the planet. However, videos and books give us all the background knowledge we need to create a meaningful association to a word so that we can use it.

Here are several ways that description skills can be increased.

1. **Laddering** – Before we can use a word independently we have to hear the word and hear how it is used. Laddering is the process of adding one description to every word that a child says. If a child says "cookie," we say; "Yes! Two/ chocolate cookies." There is not an expectation that the child repeats what we say. We are just going up one rung of complexity to show how a word can be expanded upon.

2. **Label Classroom or Household Objects** - Using post-it notes to label items is a great way to introduce young children to the words in their environment. Older children can do the labeling for you!

3. **Engage Your Child in Story Telling** – Stories become interesting when they are rich in description. Encourage your child to share a story about something that happened in their life or a story that they have made up on their own. Be sure to ask leading questions that require describing. For example, "You said they were at the North Pole. What was it like there and what did it feel like?"

4. **Converse Regularly** – Just like with story-telling, conversation improves vocabulary and description skills because it provides more opportunity to practice. Also, people like to be listened to. Creating an engaging (descriptive) conversation makes people want to listen to us.

5. **Play with Words** – Here a many different word games that are fun and promote

Teaching How to Describe　　　　　　7.4

learning. Scrabble is one of the most popular. It is a high level game but there is a whole range of other games for all different levels. Check out: Boggle, Hangman, Apples to Apples, 7 Little Words, What's the Word, and Word Stack. There are also games that don't require anything physical, like the Alphabet game played in the car where you need to find a word starting with each letter in alphabetical order.

6. **Don't be Afraid of Bigger Vocabulary** – Studies have shown that children whose parents used "rare words" had higher vocabularies and greater reading achievement than other children. We want to engage children on their own level but that doesn't mean that they can't benefit from being around age-level vocabulary or higher. All vocabulary that is successfully used was first heard being used by someone else in their environment or on television.

7. **Read to Children** – As we move along the continuum of how to increase description skills we finally arrive at reading. Reading to a child is a powerful way to demonstrate describing. Children hear words and make connections to the pictures. They hear the correct pronunciation of the word, and the many ways the word can be used. They are actively engaged in the story so the word is better able to be imprinted to memory. Reading to children is an obvious strategy. However, make sure that you are reading both storybooks and informational books. Parents and teachers tend to emphasize vocabulary more when they read informational books.

8. **Increase Word Consciousness** – Children should notice when they come across a new word and be excited to share it with you. The last thing we want is for a child to encounter a new word and feel embarrassed because they don't know what it means. We can help with this process by pointing out when we encounter new words too. Let your child share in the process of learning new word meanings with you.

9. **Teach Across Multiple Contexts** - Create opportunities for the same words to be used across multiple activities, conversations, and texts. For example, words

Teaching How to Describe

related to the five senses can be discussed at lunch as well as during science class.

The words that we learn are based on our experiences and the many associations we make between a word and its relationship to our other experiences. The more associations we have with a word, the better we are able to remember it, retrieve it, and use it. As we strengthen our associations with a word, the use of the word will come along naturally. A child might need to hear a word many times and have many different experiences with it before they fully grasp the concept and add it to their word repertoire. This is completely normal. Children develop at their own pace. We need to honor each child's pace and encourage their learning.

Describing Activity 7.4

In the Car/En el Carro

Draw a line from each type of transportation and describe WHERE it belongs.

Dibuje una línea desde cada tipo de transporte y describe DONDE viaja.

SESSION 8

Shopping

Ir de compras

SHOPPING   8

SPEECH AND LANGUAGE SESSION FOCUS

CATEGORIZATION

As interventionists we are constantly grouping things. In a clinical setting or with a favorite set of manipulatives, we can sort objects by size or color. The average parent may not spend as much time actively thinking about the process of categorization. Luckily, the grocery store is the perfect setting for focusing on this skill. First and foremost the categories are named (e.g., dairy, produce). They are broken down into subsets (e.g., vegetables, fruits). They are grouped by attributes (e.g., fresh vegetables, frozen vegetables). Finally, they are put in an order (e.g., big things go on the bottom shelf). Parents report that they can be overwhelmed by vocabulary and speech knowledge when they are beginning to learn how to help their child communicate. Rather than extolling the virtues of teaching categories, attributes, and functions, champion what parents naturally do in a grocery store. By applying categorization to such a familiar setting, the parent may have a greater understanding of its purpose, and subsequently, apply the idea to the rest of their day.

TODAY'S PLAN

Parents should be encouraged to:

- Ask a child where he/she might find something from the shopping list. For example, "We need eggs. Where are they? Yes, they are in the dairy section."
- Joke with the child by calling an object by the wrong name and see if he/she names it correctly.
- Name each object before putting it in the cart.
- Ask a child to help find some of his/her favorite things. For example, "Here is the cereal, do you see your loopies?"

Routines-Based Early Intervention Guidebook

SHOPPING 8.1

Sign	Use signs and words together. **Up Store Bag**
Model	Use simple phrases. **"Big apple" "Get eggs"**
Imitate	Imitate sounds, signs, words, and gestures that your child uses. **Say, "mmm" when you buy a favorite food**
Label	Name objects in your child's environment. **Name items as you put them in your cart.**
Expand	Add words to what your child says. **When your child says "Ice cream," You say, "Cold ice cream."**

Practice these important words and add more of your own:

FOOD	MEAT	_____
EGGS	CHICKEN	_____
BREAD	VEGETABLES	_____
SOUP	FRUIT	_____
I LIKE	YOGURT	_____

SHOPPING

ACTIVITY IDEAS:
- Pretend to shop at home using real cans and packages of food or plastic toys and have your child put them in a basket while labeling them.

- Practice using location words to describe where food items are in the store (e.g., "up high," "down below," "on the shelf").

- Group food items into categories: dairy, meat, fruits, vegetables.

I will help my child by:

- _____
- _____

My child will:

_____
_____
_____
_____

THERAPIST SUGGESTS:

What happened?
- What did you do?
- What did your child say or do?
- What questions do you have?

_____
_____
_____

Ir de Compras

SEÑALAR	Junte señas y palabras. **Arriba** **Tienda** **Bolsa**
OFRECER **M**ODELOS	Diga frases sencillas. "La manzana grande" "¿Qué es?"
NOMBRAR	Nombre objetos en su ambiente. "Pan" "Huevos"
REPETIR **I**MITAR	Repita sonidos, señas, palabras, y gestos que usa su niño/a. **Digale, "mmm" cuando compre una comida que le guste.**
EXTENDER	Añada palabras a lo que dice su niño/a. **Cuando su niño/a diga "Helado," usted dígale, "Helado frío."**

Practiquen estas palabras importantes y agreguen más:

COMIDA	CARNE	_____
HUEVOS	POLLO	_____
PAN	VERDURAS	_____
SOPA	FRUTA	_____
ME GUSTA	YOGUR	_____

Ir de Compras

IDEAS DE ACTIVIDADES:
- Simule ir de compras en casa con latas y paquetes de alimentos reales o con juguetes de plástico. Haga que su niño/a las ponga en una canasta mientras las nombra.

- Practique usando palabras de ubicación, para describir donde están los alimentos en la tienda (por ejemplo, "arriba," "abajo," "en el estante").

- Agrupe los alimentos en categorías: lácteos, carne, frutas, verduras.

Ayudaré a mi niño/a así:

- _____
- _____

Mi niño/a va a:

_____
_____
_____
_____

> Sugerencia de la Terapista:

¿Qué pasó?
- ¿Qué hizo Ud.?
- ¿Qué dijo o hizo su niño/a?
- ¿Qué preguntas tiene Ud.?

_____
_____
_____
_____

Shopping/Ir de Compras 8.3

Signs/Señas

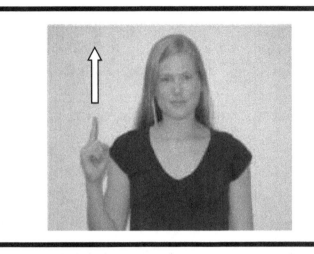
Up / Arriba

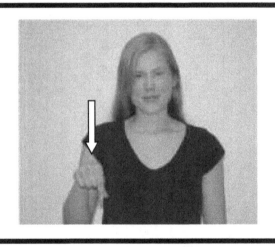
Down / Abajo

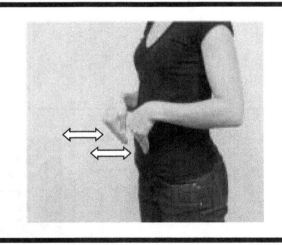
Store / Tienda

Shopping/Ir de Compras

Teaching Categorization   8.4

As a child's vocabulary begins to grow, categorization is an important feature. It helps children organize their knowledge in different ways, which ultimately helps them retrieve the words they want to use and express their ideas. Think of building a categorization structure like building a web of words. The more ways the word is connected to your structure, the easier it is to pull up when you want to use it. It is important for children to understand that there are many different ways to group objects. This will help them grow their vocabularies.

Understanding a bit about the science behind categorization helps us understand the importance of working and why to work on building categories, rather than just working on vocabulary. Think of categorization in terms of your desk or your computer desktop. If you receive a bill, chances are you have a folder to put that bill in. But what about the random things you receive that sit on your desktop. Let's say you have a mortgage document from buying a new house. You have no need for a folder (aka category) for that document until you have more than one piece of information relating to it. Your bill folder might be huge and something you access all the time. Or, your folder with mortgage documents might become full quickly but then you may not look at it again for a long time.

Language categories grow the same way. A child learns a word such as "doggie." All furry, small, four-legged things are "doggie" until she meets a "doggie" that doesn't match the category well. Let's say she goes to a farm. Now she has these other words and needs a group called "animals." Another common example for young children is that all men are "daddy" or all women are "mommy" until they start to differentiate between uncle, aunt, sister, brother, etc. Then a group develops. In the beginning, all colors may be red or all shapes are circles until we differentiate between the two and we need new names and a group. Once the group (the category) is established, a child's vocabulary typically grows like wildfire and they fill it with an uncountable number of objects. When vocabulary growth is delayed or does not follow the natural course, we can speed up vocabulary acquisition by building and strengthening categorization skills. Children typically learn categorization through natural interactions in their environment and this is the best way to teach categorization to children who are struggling.

Categorization is the organization of our environment: e.g. rooms in our house,

Teaching Categorization

sections of a supermarket, centers in a classroom. Categorization allows us to describe: e.g. colors, shapes, sizes, temperature, number. Categorization enables us to differentiate: e.g. animals that fly, crawl, walk, have feathers, have skin, have hair. Categorization also lets us talk about things we have not learned the name of yet. This is called circumlocution and we all use this strategy. For example, "You know that animal that's a bird, but it doesn't fly, and it lives where it is cold. What is called? A penguin!" Let's begin with a hierarchy of categorization skills and then we'll share some activities.

Categorization Skill Hierarchy

- Match objects to their pictures
- Match objects that are the same (two identical pictures)
- Sort a small number of objects into two groups (red and green)
- Sort a group of objects by one feature (all red objects)
- Choose an object and place it in one of many categories based on name or attribute (color)
- Sort multiple objects into multiple categories (cleaning up toys)
- Name categories (these are all....)
- Name the category of an animal (a dog is an animal)
- Provide names of objects when given a category (tell me all of the X you can think of)
- Express similarities and differences that enable something to be categorized
- Tell why an object *doesn't* belong in a category (because those are all fish and this is a bird)

Teaching categorization skills is the process of identifying where your child falls on the hierarchy, improving those skills and then moving up to the next level of difficulty.

Categorization Activities

1. **Book Reading** – There are many great fiction and non-fiction books showing

Teaching Categorization   8.4

categories. Nothing special has to be done when reading them. Just make sure to frequently include this genre of books with all your other favorites. Some examples include:

- Books that name mother and baby animals: horse/colt/foal, cow/calf, sheep/lamb, dog/puppy, cat/kitten.
- Books that describe attributes of a single category: animals by color, animals by sizes.
- Books that name objects found in specific places: furniture in different rooms of the house, tools and buildings found on a farm, businesses found along Main Street, items found in various sections of the grocery store, and so on.

2. **Sorting activities** – Sorting activities are best begun with physical objects. If you are at a school, math manipulatives are perfect as they have a high number of similar objects used for counting. It is best not to have two variables initially. For instance, use the colored bears in the math manipulatives to sort by color. Don't use the colored animals to sort by color because a child could put all of the animals together, all of the colors, or a combination of the both. If you start by sorting animals, make sure they are all the same color.

3. **Similarities and Differences** – The first categorization skill that is usually taught in school is "same and different." For children who are struggling with categorization, this is still a great activity but make sure not to jump up to WHY questions too soon. Talk out loud about why things are grouped but allow the child to make her own inferences.

4. **Sort by Attribute** – Building blocks are perfect for sorting by size, color, or shape. Again, for struggling learners or very young children, only focus on one attribute at a time. Building towers is really exciting for children because they love to knock it down. Towards the top, request specific blocks that you will add so that the tower gets taller. This tests their receptive language skills (understanding).

5. **Location, Location, Location** – Objects belong in a certain place. Whether it is around the house or the classroom. Children can help clean up or retrieve objects.

Teaching Categorization

At its essence, a room in a house or a classroom station *is* a category. Create treasure hunt lists for a child to collect random objects. You can also race a child to a predetermined object.

6. Grocery shopping – The grocery store is the ultimate category location. Each food is subdivided into departments. As you shop, you can talk about everything in each section and why they go together. A child can also make a shopping list of her favorite items and locate them as you move through the store. Don't forget to use your little helper at home to unpack the groceries and put them away in the correct categorical place. This is a good opportunity to have some fun. Put boxed goods in the fridge and ice cream in the oven. Let the child "correct you" to demonstrate her knowledge.

7. Likes and Dislikes – Children can create a board that is subdivided into TV shows, activities, and even foods that define who they are and what they prefer. This is a categorization activity that links to building empathy as we develop an understanding of what others around us prefer or fear.

8. Create a categorization book – a quick search for any category will produce a ton of pictures on the internet. These pictures can be cut up and mixed into many categories. The child can then paste each picture on its appropriate category page.

A little bit of focus on categorization skills goes a long way. When children are finally able to identify the common property of a group without being reminded, you have enhanced their vocabulary and thinking!

Categorization Activity

Shopping/Ir de compras

8.4

Talk about what foods you need to buy at the store and make a list. You can tape photos of products from advertisements or parts of boxes to the list also. Where in the store do you find the food? What group is it in?

Hable sobre las comidas que tiene que comprar en la tienda y póngalas en una lista. Puede pegar fotos de productos de los anuncios o partes de cajas a la lista también. ¿Dónde en la tienda encuentra la comida? ¿En cuál grupo está?

My Shopping List!
¡Mi lista de compras!

Food/ Comida	What words or gestures did your child use? / ¿Cuáles palabras o gestos usó su niño/a?	
Bananas/ Plátanos	*Pointed at the bananas/ Indicó los plátanos*	☑
[cereal box image]	*Said "ohs"/Dijo "Os"*	☑

Session 9

At Home

En la Casa

At Home

Speech and Language Session Focus

Labeling

On the surface, labeling can simply be seen as the naming of objects. Indeed, parents are happy when they ask their child, "What is this?" and they get the appropriate response. However, parents can also grow frustrated when they ask their child to say a word many times (e.g., "Say 'dog.' Dog. Woof-woof. Now you say it.") without success.

Parents normally love the process of teaching words, and we, as interventionists, need to teach them how to do it effectively. The more that a child hears the name of an object, the more likely he or she is to say it. The home environment provides everything that is needed to make this interaction more successful.

Today's Plan

The first part of naming an object is knowing what an object is called.

Parents should be encouraged:

- To name objects in the house in front of the child.
- Not to expect a child to name everything immediately.
- To be a good role model by frequently naming things.
- To celebrate when a child identifies an object with words like "this" and "that."

The second part of naming includes practicing saying the names of objects.

Parents should:

- Begin by naming objects that are meaningful to the child.
- Ask the child to name objects that they need or really want.
- Request the words that a child is already able to use.
- Encourage hand gestures while communicating.

At Home

9.1

SIGN	Use signs and words together. **Sit**　　**Stand**　　**TV**
MODEL	Use simple phrases. **"Open door"**　　**"In your room"**
IMITATE	Imitate sounds, signs, words, and gestures that your child uses. **Imitate brushing your teeth.**
LABEL	Name objects in your child's environment. **"Stove"**　　**"Couch"**
EXPAND	Add words to what your child says. **When your child says "Chair," you say, "On chair."**

Practice these important words and add more of your own:

DOOR	WINDOW	_____
TELEVISION	KITCHEN	_____
CHAIR	ROOM	_____
SOFA	STAIRS	_____
TABLE	CLEAN UP	_____

AT HOME

ACTIVITY IDEAS:
- Play hide and seek with a toy by placing it in different locations and asking yes/no questions: "Is it under the chair?" "Is it on the table?"

- Talk about the functions of objects in the home (e.g., brush teeth with a toothbrush, write with a pen, cut with scissors, eat with a fork).

- Have your child help you clean up and talk about where things go in the house by labeling the rooms: kitchen, bathroom, bedroom, etc.

I will help my child by:

- _____
- _____

My child will:

_____
_____
_____
_____

THERAPIST SUGGESTS:

What happened?

- What did you do?
- What did your child say or do?
- What questions do you have?

_____
_____
_____
_____

En la Casa

9.2

SONRÍE	
Señalar	Junte señas y palabras. **Sentarse Levantarse Televisión**
Ofrecer Modelos	Diga frases sencillas. **"Abre la puerta" "En las escaleras"**
Nombrar	Nombre objetos en su ambiente. **"Estufa" "Sofá"**
Repetir	Repita sonidos, señas, palabras, y gestos que usa su niño/a.
Imitar	**Imite a su niño/a cuando se cepille los dientes.**
Extender	Añada palabras a lo que dice su niño/a. **Cuando su niño/a diga "Silla," usted dígale, "En la silla."**

Practiquen estas palabras importantes y agreguen más:

PUERTA	VENTANA	_____
TELEVISIÓN	COCINA	_____
SILLA	CUARTO	_____
SOFÁ	ESCALERAS	_____
MESA	LIMPIAR	_____

En la Casa

IDEAS DE ACTIVIDADES:

- Juegue a las escondidas con un juguete, colocándolo en diferentes lugares y haga preguntas cuyas respuestas sean sí o no: "¿Está debajo de la silla?" "¿Está encima de la mesa?"

- Hable de las funciones de los objetos en la casa (por ejemplo, lavarse los dientes con un cepillo de dientes, escribir con un lápiz, cortar con tijeras, comer con un tenedor).

- Deje que su niño/a le ayude a recoger la casa y explíquele dónde van las cosas, dándole nombre a las diferentes áreas: cocina, baño, dormitorio, etc.

Ayudaré a mi niño/a así:

- _____
- _____

Mi niño/a va a:

_____
_____
_____
_____

> Sugerencia de la Terapista:

¿Qué pasó?

- ¿Qué hizo Ud.?
- ¿Qué dijo o hizo su niño/a?
- ¿Qué preguntas tiene Ud.?

_____
_____
_____

Routines-Based Early Intervention Guidebook

At Home/En La Casa 9.3

Signs/Señas

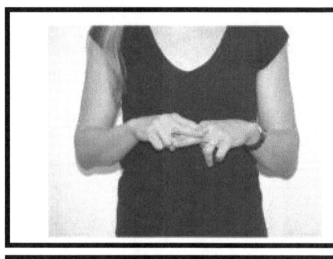

Sit
Sentarse

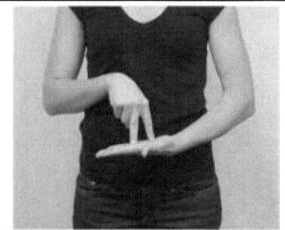

Stand
Levantarse

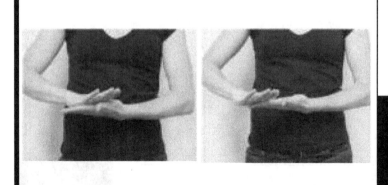

Clean up
Limpiar

At Home/En La Casa

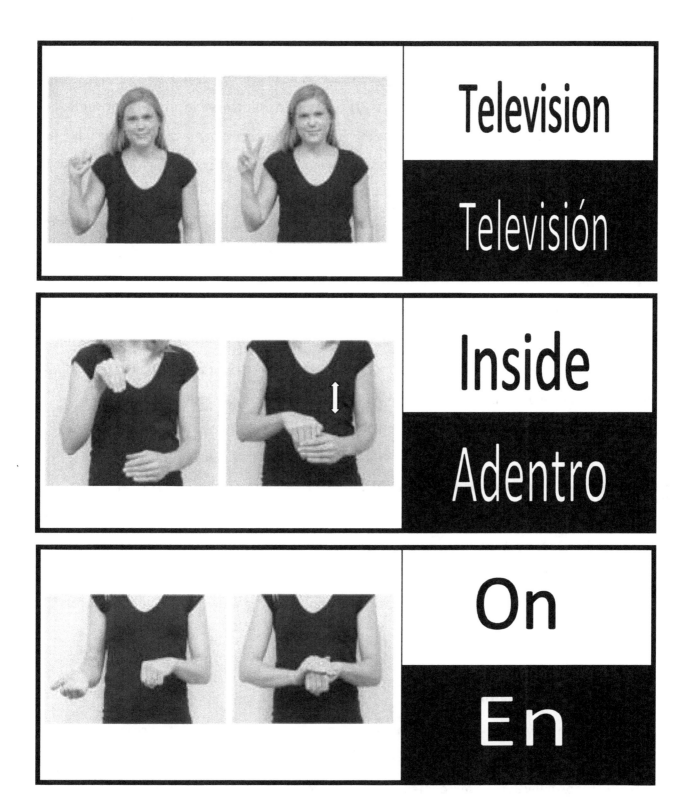

Teaching Labeling Skills   9.4

When we think about a child's vocabulary, we are in large part describing a child's success at remembering and naming objects. These names (labels) that we put on an object are arbitrary. For instance, there is no reason why the sounds D+U+K couldn't mean table, or house, rather than an animal that says, "Quack!" Certainly, in other languages D+U+K does not mean duck. We have simply all agreed to label objects in a certain way to make communication and understanding possible. This is why learning new vocabulary for some children is difficult. There is no exact reason why an object has the name it has, so we have to increase our knowledge about the object and use high repetition in order to remember what it is called.

Successful activities that increase a child's labeling skills are packed with examples and repetition, but not demands. For example, when a child points to an orange to express that he wants it, we can say, "Oh, orange. You want the orange." I often hear parents say, "Say orange," and even say, "You can have it after you say orange." We want language learning to be fun, and one thing we know is that children will say the words when they are ready to do so. It can be a great source of frustration for a child who wants an orange to have the orange withheld because he cannot say that word yet. Such frustration can lead to a diminished desire to communicate. Remember to applaud your child's communication even if it is nonverbal or unclear, and to help with their language growth by labeling the objects and actions in your child's environment. You might feel like you sound like a broken record at times but remember that the more your child hears words, the sooner he will learn them, and the sooner he we say them.

As educators and parents, we do a pretty good job at teaching new vocabulary. However, there are few unique strategies that can enhance the growth of labeling skills for children at any level.

Labeling Activities and Ideas

1. **Role Play** – Books, movies, and toys give us to opportunity to act as characters, change our name, and interact with a variety of imaginary objects that aren't normally in our environment. For example, playing pirate gives you access to all

TEACHING LABELING SKILLS

the words needed for burying treasure and living on a ship.

2. **Interact with Older Children** – Older children have more developed vocabularies. Younger children naturally want to fit in and love spending time with older children. By creating events that cross-pollinate age groups we have organic exposure to a larger use of vocabulary. Some school models such as Montessori are designed to mix ages. Elementary schools often have reading-buddy programs where older classes pair up with younger classrooms. Additionally, some schools offer mentoring from the older students. If a child or student has limited vocabulary, these are great opportunities to naturally have their labeling skills expand.

3. **Increase Exposure to New Toys and Objects–** This is easier at school than at home as new toys, objects, and books are swapped out with the weekly change of themes. Teachers should know that children with low vocabulary skills might require longer exposure to an object to be able to name it. Parents should know that frequent trips to the library or creating a toy exchange with friends can greatly enhance their child's naming abilities. A great way to merge the home and school environment is to have the teacher send some objects home the week after she is finished using them for teaching. This gives the child the opportunity to practice his new words with his parents. The parents can exchange the objects each Monday for the next set of words.

4. **Use Many Descriptive Words** – When an object is named alongside a descriptive word (brown cat), the object label is reinforced because it stays the same while the descriptive word changes and enhances the child's understanding of the word. Brown cat becomes, big cat, mean cat, one cat, old cat, or walking cat which creates further understanding of the word cat.

5. **Emphasize New Words** – When a child uses a new word or correctly labels an object for the first time, make a big deal of it. This lets her know that naming objects is important and she will be on the lookout for opportunities to label objects and receive praise again.

Routines-Based Early Intervention Guidebook

TEACHING LABELING SKILLS 9.4

6. **Place Printed Words Throughout Their Environment** – Printed words, even for children who are not yet reading, emphasize that all objects have labels. These can be name cards taped to any object in the room. This can be a word wall of all new vocabulary that accompanies pictures. This can also be a child's word—his name, and a picture of him and his class.

Labeling objects is something that you are probably already doing with your student or child. Get the maximum benefit from these activities by making the new words important, by integrating new words into a child's current play and daily experiences, and by naturally weaving them in and out of conversations.

Labeling Activity
At Home/En la casa

Take turns choosing each object and then let the child find it in the house. Cross each object out after you find it.

Tome turnos escogiendo un objeto y pida que su niño/a lo encuentre en la casa. Táchelo después de encontrarlo.

Session 10

Bathtime

Bañarse

BATHTIME   10

Speech and Language Session Focus

Imitation

To a parent, imitation is often thought of as copying a body movement or repeating a phrase, "Say _____." However, imitation is a two-way street. It is just as important for us to repeat what a child says as it is for them to repeat what we say. This is their feedback to know if they have successfully said or did what you asked of them. We are familiar with all of the speech components involved in saying a word. Proper volume, resonance (i.e., the use of the nose and the mouth), rhythm, and intonation (i.e., raising and lowering your voice) all must be present along with the sounds that make up the word. When all these aspects are present, we say that a child repeated a word or imitated what we said correctly. Sharing the complexities of oral speech is very important for parents to know because they can still be working on supporting skills like imitating sounds or facial movements even though their child may not be speaking yet. This way, parents and teachers celebrate small triumphs while still building a base for communication.

Bath time is a great opportunity to practice imitation It takes place in an acoustically confined space and provides one-on-one time without other distractions. Songs can be used during this routine to provide all the necessary aspects of speech without getting too technical. Moreover, children love music and few things are more motivational.

Today's Plan

Use the bath time routine to identify a child's communicative strengths. Use these as a base to begin to build speech and to motivate the parent.

Encourage the parent to:

- Use songs if a child is not speaking. Single sounds or single syllables could be out of a child's range for a starting point.
- Sing or hum with a child during any daily activity.
- Use songs that contain linguistic concepts (e.g., "Itsy Bitsy Spider," "Head, Shoulders, Knees, and Toes"). Made-up songs are great too!

Routines-Based Early Intervention Guidebook

Bathtime 10.1

SIGN	Use signs and words together. **Wash** **Duck** **Bubbles**
MODEL	Use simple phrases. **"Wash face"** **"Put toys in"**
IMITATE	Imitate sounds, signs, words, and gestures that your child uses. **Imitate songs or toy noises.**
LABEL	Name objects in your child's environment. **"Soap"** **"Bathtub"**
EXPAND	Add words to what your child says. When your child says "Duck," you say, "Yellow Duck."

Practice these important words and add more of your own:

DUCK	DIRTY	_____
TOWEL	CLEAN	_____
WATER	FACE	_____
BUBBLES	HANDS	_____
SOAP	TOYS	_____

BATHTIME

ACTIVITY IDEAS:
- Have your child pretend to give his/her doll or toy a bath. Have your child wash different parts of the doll/toy to target learning names of body parts (e.g., "wash hair," "wash feet").

- Ask your child what he/she will wash next to encourage labeling of body parts.

- Sing "Head, Shoulders, Knees and Toes" while washing in the tub.

I will help my child by:

- _____
- _____

My child will:

_____
_____
_____
_____

THERAPIST SUGGESTS:

What happened?

-What did you do?
-What did your child say or do?
-What questions do you have?

_____
_____
_____
_____

Bañarse

SEÑALAR	Junte señas y palabras. **Lavar Pato Burbujas**
OFRECER **M**ODELOS	Diga frases sencillas. **"Lava la cara" "Pon juguetes"**
NOMBRAR	Nombre objetos en su ambiente. **"Jabón" "Toalla"**
REPETIR	Repita sonidos, señas, palabras, y gestos que usa su niño/a. **Cante con su niño/a o haga sonidos de juguetes.**
IMITAR **E**XTENDER	Añada palabras a lo que dice su niño/a. **Cuando su niño/a diga "Pato" usted dígale, "El pato nada."**

Practiquen estas palabras importantes y agreguen más:

PATO	SUCIO/SUCIA	_____
TOALLA	LIMPIO/LIMPIA	_____
AGUA	CARA	_____
BURBUJAS	MANOS	_____
JABÓN	JUGUETES	_____

BAÑARSE

IDEAS DE ACTIVIDADES:
- Ponga a su niño/a a simular que baña a su muñeco o juguete. Pídale que le lave diferentes partes a la muñeca o juguete para que aprenda los nombres de las partes del cuerpo (por ejemplo, "lávale el cabello," "lávale los pies").

- Pregúntele a su niño/a que parte le va a lavar después, para estimularlo a nombrar las partes del cuerpo.

- Canten "Cabeza, hombros, rodillas y pies" mientras se baña en la bañera.

Ayudaré a mi niño/a así:

- _____
- _____

Mi niño/a va a:

_____
_____
_____

> SUGERENCIA DE LA TERAPISTA:

¿Qué pasó?

- ¿Qué hizo Ud.?
- ¿Qué dijo o hizo su niño/a?
- ¿Qué preguntas tiene Ud.?

_____
_____
_____

Bathtime/Bañarse

10.3

Signs/Señas

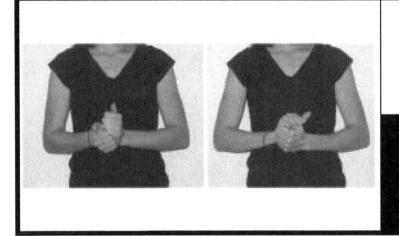

Wash

Lavarse

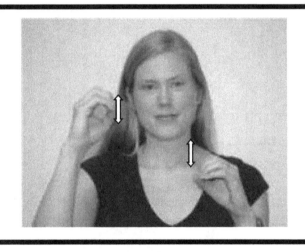

Bubbles

Burbujas

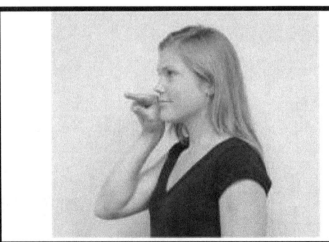

Duck

Pato

Bathtime/Bañarse

Teaching Imitation Skills 10.4

Imitation is the basis for all learning. From the timeless advice that "practice makes perfect" to the updated version that "perfect practice makes perfect," we are encouraged to imitate in order to learn. Think back to any event in your life. Whether it was speaking, reading, or writing, multiple sessions had to occur before you internalized the ability or knowledge and began using it effortlessly. Now, truly try to remember one of those learning events. Did you hate it? Chances are you were engrossed in every second of it which added to the triumph of the accomplishment. The ability to reproduce the motions or words of another person is mandatory for learning. For the person learning, it is an enjoyable process.

This is a very important point because for children with language delays, research tells us that they need to hear words many, many more times than children with typical development. While we as adults might get bored when the child requests to reread a book for the tenth time or play a game infinitely, children love repetition and crave the success they experience from recognition and understanding. If you as a parent or teacher are guilty of hiding one of these games or books, you are not alone! With children who have difficulty imitating words or simple actions, we can lean on this innate love to teach a child how to successfully repeat.

As with any new skills, different children require different levels of support and repetition to learn them. It is our job to identify the level at which a child is successfully able to repeat an action and then slowly increase the level of difficulty over time.

Activities to Improve Imitation Skills

1. **Teachable Moments** – It should first be noted that we are not adding anything new to our daily schedule to improve imitation skills. Whether you are cooking, making the bed, writing, or walking in the hall, have your child imitate your actions. Use these daily activities that already occur as opportunities to have a child repeat your actions, movements, or words.
2. **Singing and Dancing** – The kinesthetic movements and sensory involvement of singing and dancing enables learning to involve the entire brain. The music and

TEACHING IMITATION SKILLS

movements create cues which at their essence are complex multi-step routines. You can slow a song down or teach it in segments until a child is able to follow along on their own.

3. **Board Games** – With the advent of new technologies, physical games with real boards and moveable pieces are becoming increasingly rare. Games are repetitious by their very nature and players tend to do the same thing over-and-over each turn. Once they learn the rules, children often play games independently. This has the added benefit of freeing up your schedule and rewarding their independence.

4. **Book Reading** – Repetition is skillfully used in the development of books for young children to maintain their interest, support their developing fluency, and teach academic concepts. Books are best described when looking at them through the eyes of the children who are reading them.

   Toddlers – Book-*reading* with very young children would be more appropriately called book-*exploration*. They turn the book backwards and forwards, up and down, swim through multiple pages, or spend an infinity on one image. Young children are as captivated by the experience as they are by the content. This exploration helps them understand what everything is and understand what the relation is between all of the objects present. Part of the reason for young children requesting that the same book be read over-and-over is because they are developing a sense of expectation and it thrills them to be able to predict what is coming next. Join your child in this exploration. Imitate the characters, sounds that things in the picture would make, and try to drop any preconceived notions about what "book-reading" looks like at this age.

   Preschool Children – Preschoolers reading books depend heavily on the repetitious nature of this genre of books. The very best rhymes have repeated images and phrases, and repeat one main word on each page. For example, *Brown Bear – Brown Bear* is repeated on every page of Eric Carle's classic while the animals that the bear sees change by name, color, and image. The repetitive nature of these books acts as scaffolding that allows the preschooler to access more

Teaching Imitation Skills

advanced content even though their reading skills are not fully developed. The repetitious nature creates a familiarity so that the child knows what is next and can imitate you while reading or act out the movements of the characters. If you are working with a 4-year-old or older child who is behind, repetitive and predictable books are a great place to begin.

School-age Children – By the time a child has entered school, books layer academic themes across the stories narrative. Size, numbers, letters, colors, shapes, and emotions can be rapidly introduced by reading a single text. Whole categories of animals or any vocabulary topic are at our fingertips. A true demonstration of a book's teaching power lies in the ease with which a child recites whole passages by the second time they are reading it. Grade school books *are* highly repetitive but they also allow a child to practice and apply what they learned in school when they are paired with academic themes. For school-age children, send a book home that matches what is being taught. If you are a parent, ask a teacher what is being taught each week and hit the library to allow for carryover at home.

IMITATION ACTIVITY

BATHTIME/BAÑARSE

Use these songs during real or pretend bath time to help a child repeat what you say.

Utilice estas canciones durante el tiempo real del baño o juegue como si estuviera bañándose para ayudar a un niño a repetir lo que dice.

THE ITSY BITSY SPIDER	LA ARAÑA PEQUEÑITA
The itsy bitsy spider climbed up the water spout Down came the rain and washed the spider out Out came the sun and dried up all the rain And the itsy bitsy spider climbed up the spout again	La araña pequeñita subió, subió, subió Vino la lluvia y se la llevó Salió el sol y todo lo secó Y la araña pequeñita subió, subió, subió
ROW YOUR BOAT	VAMOS A REMAR
Row, row, row your boat Gently down the stream Merrily, merrily, merrily, merrily Life is but a dream	Ven, ven, ven acá Vamos a remar Rema, que rema, que rema, que rema Me tienes que ayudar
HEAD, SHOULDERS, KNEES, AND TOES	CABEZA, HOMBROS, RODILLAS Y PIES
Head, shoulders, knees, and toes, knees and toes Head, shoulders, knees, and toes, knees and toes Eyes and ears and mouth and nose Head, shoulders, knees, and toes, knees and toes	Cabeza, hombros, rodillas y pies, rodillas y pies Cabeza, hombros, rodillas y pies, rodillas y pies Ojos, orejas, boca y nariz Cabeza, hombros, rodillas y pies, rodillas y pies
ELENA WAS A WHALE	ELENA LA BALLENA
Elena, Elena, Elena was a whale She lived, she lived, she lived out in the sea In the deep blue sea, how she liked to swim In the deep blue sea, how she liked to play How deep! How deep! How deep! How deep! How deep is the deep blue sea!	Elena, Elena, Elena la ballena Vivía, vivía, vivía allá en el mar En el agua azul, le gustaba nadar En el agua azul, le gustaba jugar ¡Qué hondo! ¡Qué hondo! ¡Qué hondo es el mar! ¡Qué hondo! ¡Qué hondo! ¡Qué hondo es el mar!

Session 11

Storytime

Tiempo de leer

STORYTIME

Speech and Language Session Focus

Contrasting

The higher-level language skills of comparing and contrasting, identifying opposites, and stating an opinion can be boiled down to a decision between *yes* and *no*. Mentally we calculate whether we *DO* or *DON'T* like something or whether something *DOES* or *DOESN'T* have similar attributes. When a child is not understood, learning how to nod for "yes" or shake his or her head for "no" is powerful. For the parent, learning how to ask yes/no questions is equally powerful. Toddlers with disabilities often say "yes" or "no" but not both.

Storytime provides many opportunities to compare and contrast pictures and concepts, thereby enabling the child to participate in book reading. The child can describe actions (open/close book) or identify the pictures/objects on the page.

Today's Plan

This intervention session should be used to establish if and how a child says "yes" and/or "no." Does he or she say the words or just move his/her head or both? Is it only when he or she is angry, or sad, or when he or she just wants something? Practice the difference between asking yes/no questions and "wh" questions so that parents understand the difference.

Parents should be encouraged to:

- Move their own heads when they say "yes" and "no" even if they are not accustomed to it.
- Use yes/no questions before "wh" questions.
- Request that a child responds at least with a head shake when asked a question.
- Model "yes" and "no" with questions. For example, "Do you want this book? Yes? (nod)."

Storytime

Sign	Use signs and words together. **Book** **Open** **Again**
Model	Use simple phrases. **"Open book"** **"Turn the page"**
Imitate	Imitate sounds, signs, words, and gestures that your child uses. **Imitate child's reactions to the story.**
Label	Name objects in your child's environment. **"Book" "Page"**
Expand	Add words to what your child says. **When your child says "Book" you say, "Read book"**

Practice these important words and add more of your own:

BOOK	OPEN	_____
READ	CLOSE	_____
WHO	DO	_____
WHAT	WHERE	_____
PAGE	ALL DONE	_____

STORYTIME

ACTIVITY IDEAS:

- Set up a story corner in your home where you and your child can read together. Let your child choose a book and look at the pictures together before you read it.

- Talk with your child about the parts of the book. Label the title, author, illustrator, front and back covers, and the pages.

- Take your child to the library. Pick two books on topics that your child will like (e.g., dinosaurs, princesses). Hold up the two books and ask your child which book he/she wants to read. Sit down and read the book.

I will help my child by:

- _____
- _____

My child will:

_____
_____
_____
_____

THERAPIST SUGGESTS:

What happened?

-What did you do?
-What did your child say or do?
-What questions do you have?

_____
_____
_____
_____

Tiempo de Leer

11.2

Señalar	Junte señas y palabras. **Libro** **Abrir** **Otra vez**
Ofrecer **M**odelos	Diga frases sencillas. **"Abre libro"** **"Cambia la página"**
Nombrar	Nombre objetos en el ambiente. **"Libro"** **"Página"**
Repetir **Í**mitar	Repita sonidos, señas, palabras, y gestos que usa su niño/a. **Imite lo que hace su niño/a cuando reaccione al libro.**
Extender	Añada palabras a lo que dice su niño/a. **Cuando su niño/a diga "Libro" usted dígale, "Leer un libro."**

Practiquen estas palabras importantes y agreguen más:

LIBRO	ABRIR	_____
LEER	CERRAR	_____
QUIÉN	HACER	_____
QUÉ	DÓNDE	_____
PÁGINA	SE ACABÓ	_____

Tiempo de Leer

IDEAS DE ACTIVIDADES:
- Establezca un rincón de lectura en su casa donde usted y su niño/a puedan leer juntos. Deje que su niño/a elija un libro y vean juntos las ilustraciones antes de leerlo.

- Hable con su niño/a acerca de las partes del libro. Nómbrele la portada, el título, el autor, el ilustrador, la cubierta anterior y posterior, y las páginas.

- Lleve a su niño/a a la biblioteca pública. Elija dos libros de temas que su niño/a prefiere (por ejemplo, dinosaurios, princesas). Sostenga los dos libros y pregúntele a su niño/a cual quiere leer. Siéntense y lean el libro.

Ayudaré a mi niño/a así:

- _____
- _____

Mi niño/a va a:

_____
_____
_____
_____

Sugerencia de la Terapista:

¿Qué pasó?
- ¿Qué hizo Ud.?
- ¿Qué dijo o hizo su niño/a?
- ¿Qué preguntas tiene Ud.?

_____
_____
_____
_____

Story Time/Tiempo de Leer   11.3

Signs/Señas

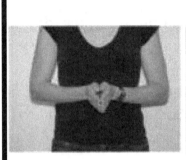 

Book

Libro

Turn page

Voltea la página

Again

Otra vez

Story Time/Tiempo de Leer

Teaching Contrasting Skills   11.4

The ability to compare an object or activity to another is a very powerful communicative ability. Even as adults, we do not remember or know everything about everything. We speak in metaphors and say things like "You know, it's that thing that's like a wolf but it's actually in the cat family. It lives in Africa, I think, or is it Australia? It always looks like it's laughing. They were the bad guys in the movie The Lion King." "Do you mean a hyena?" "Yes!" For those of us who have studied a foreign language, contrasting abilities probably made up 50% of your communication when your second-language abilities were not that strong.

Contrasting gives us the ability to lean on descriptive words, prior knowledge, metaphors, and all forms of media to try to get our point across. It gives us power because we can get our needs met, add to conversations, answer questions, and share our knowledge while our communication is limited. When children lack the ability to compare and contrast, their language can appear extremely limited. If they don't know the exact answer to a question, they don't answer at all. They don't often explain. They don't often predict, ponder, or guess. We can dramatically enhance their communication by teaching them how to access their descriptive capabilities and make positive additions to a conversation.

Contrastive thinking is one of the first patterns of thought that develops. Infants differentiate between parents, between voices, and even between tones of voice. They react emotionally to what they perceive as positive or negative and instinctively display the appropriate emotion. As children enter school, great attention is paid to a child's ability to compare and contrast because comparative thinking had the greatest effect on student achievement. Being able to compare and contrast also leads to epiphanies as students use their knowledge to come up with answers independently. Hopefully it is plain to see how important contrasting abilities are. In order to teach contrasting abilities, we are not necessarily teaching new concepts but are instead helping a child to apply descriptive concepts to problem solving and communication.

1. **Yes/No Questions** – Yes/No questions are the easiest way to access the knowledge of child without having to rely heavily on language abilities. Secondly, if you are working with a child who has extremely limited language, the ability to say "no" is

Teaching Contrasting Skills

extremely powerful because they get to communicate what they *don't* want. For the very young or uncommunicative, start with a single object that is physically present or that you have a picture of (e.g., Do you want an apple?). Create a green/red, yes/no, or smiley face/frowny face chart for them to pick from. This can often be frustrating for a child if the object or activity that they want is not presented. We acknowledge the child's frustration and continue to work to understand them. *"I see you're upset and don't want an apple. Thank you for telling me "no." Do you want to eat? You do! Great. How about a banana? No. I am sorry that I don't know what you want today but these are your two choices."* After Yes/No question abilities are established, the child is ready to move on to choosing between two objects.

Please note: In English, we see Yes/No questions as being quite simple because they only require one of two answers which can be elicited with the shake of the head. In other languages, such as Chinese, Yes/No questions are answered with verbs or nouns and not "yes" or "no." This is fundamentally more complex than how we answer questions in English. For example:

Teacher: "Do you want to eat?"

Child: "Eat." (affirmative)

Teacher: "Do you want milk"

Child: "Not* milk." (negative)

*can be a negative prefix or negative word such as "no."

2. **Physical Contrasting Games** – Games that involve matching or grouping serve three purposes. They teach a child to identify what something is by evaluating what it is not. They enhance categorization and descriptive skills because the games are typically thematic. They also drive a child to memorize or remember patterns to be successful. We have all used Matching and Memory decks of cards in fun activities. But have you leaned on them for teaching? Rather than the cartoon or TV show versions, create matching decks for any academic concepts. Easier decks mix knowledge groups (colors, numbers, shapes…) and more difficult decks stay within

TEACHING CONTRASTING SKILLS   11.4

a single teachable field (actions, animals, community workers...). The more difficult decks require greater discerning abilities to be able to pick out really minor differences. As a parent, you can create matching games using pictures of objects in your house. As a teacher, you can create a memory deck for each of the academic theme that you can use each year.

3. **Verbal Contrasting Games** – Many simple games involve contrasting abilities such as I Spy or 21 Questions. In these games, you or other children ask comparative questions to get closer to the answer. "I spy, with my little eye, something that is pink." "Is it big or small?..." Verbal games are really underutilized as a way to pass to the time and turn the truly mundane into learning activities. Car rides, hikes, cafeteria lines, and even transitions through the hallways can keep entire groups engaged and focused.

4. **Humor** – Children are always on the receiving end of learning and it can be empowering to let them be the one to lead or correct an adult. Simply mislabel an object and watch a child burst into laughter and explain why you are wrong.

    Adult: "It's a walrus."

    Child: "No! It's a bird!"

    Adult: "How do you know?"

    Child: "Because a bird has feathers and flies, not those big teeth."

5. **Similarities and Differences** - Asking students to identify similarities and differences while they are learning increases their understanding of that content. It enables them to experience fresh insights, correct mistakes, and make new connections.

6. **Be a role model** – While talking about a subject, show your children that you are deeply analyzing the subject by comparing it to everything you know. You are explaining how one object or event fits in to the greater knowledge of the world.

7. **Extra credit extension projects** – allow students to complete "extension projects" with the topics that really excite them. Have them go home and further research other aspects of your discussion and report back to class. For example: What did other scientists get famous for? What are some other countries in Africa? What

TEACHING CONTRASTING SKILLS

are other jungle animals?

8. **Create graphic organizers** – Venn diagrams are the quintessential contrasting activity. Use a Venn diagram or any divided piece of paper to better describe an object or activity and find other objects that are similar or not.

9. **Social Comparisons** – Some really great teachers I know embed contrasting activities with math concepts and socialization concepts at the start of each week. Students are asked about their favorite color/food/toy, what they did on the weekend, what they think the weather will be like, etc. This is graphed and put on the outside wall or door. The class collectively figures which percentage of the class falls into each group and knows more about the people in their small community.

CONTRASTING ACTIVITY 11.4

STORY TIME/TIEMPO DE LEER

Ask your child to contrast the differences between pictures in a book by using yes/no questions. Help your child describe the pictures with words and signs.

Pídale a su niño que contraste las diferencias entre las imágenes en un libro usando preguntas sí / no. Ayude a su niño a describir las imágenes con palabras y signos.

| Ex: Is the dog big? | Ex: Tell me: It is small. | **What did your child say or do?** |
| Ej: Es grande el perro? | Ej: Dime: Es pequeño. | **¿Qué dijo o hizo su niño/a?** |

Big/Grande	Small/Pequeño	
Open/Abrir	Close/Cerrar	
Wet/Mojado	Dry/Seco	
Up/Arriba	Down/Abajo	
Long/Largo	Short/Corto	

	Answer / La respuesta	**What does he/she say or do?** **¿Qué dice o hace?**
My child's favorite book is... El libro favorito de mi niño/a es...		
My child does not like... A mi niño/a no le gusta...		
My child prefers books about... (e.g., princesses or dinosaurs?) ¿Mi niño/a prefiere libros sobre... (p.ej., princesas o dinosaurios?)		

SESSION 12

BEDTIME

LA HORA DE ACOSTARSE

BEDTIME   12

SPEECH AND LANGUAGE SESSION FOCUS

FOLLOWING DIRECTIONS

Individual service plans often include goals that target understanding simple directions. It is important for a child to be able to follow directions for her own safety as well as to reduce frustration. Unfortunately, children most frequently hear rapidly-fired commands in situations that demand an immediate response. These situations do not provide visual support and offer little time for teaching. While this is a necessary part of life, other opportunities are needed to practice following directions in a more controlled setting. The events that take place throughout the day offer multiple chances to show a child how to properly follow directions. Most children enjoy participating in daily activities. Frustration within the house can be reduced by letting the child "help" because the child is learning how to listen and daily tasks are being accomplished.

Bedtime provides a great opportunity for a child to follow basic, one-step directions that serve a purpose. It is also a good time to allow the child to feel like an important part of the process.

TODAY'S PLAN

Use the example of a short task to concretely identify what kind of direction a child can follow. Within this hierarchy, where is he or she functioning?

- Give (pointing to single object)
- Give cup
- Give me cup
- Give me the cup
- Give me the red cup

Explain to the parent how powerful this knowledge is and practice what could be said during different daily activities. For example, assuming two words are understood, "close door," add a third word, "close door, please."

Bedtime

12.1

Sign	Use signs and words together. **Sleep** **Bed** **Blanket**
Model	Use simple phrases. **"Pajamas on" "Lights off"**
Imitate	Imitate sounds, signs, words, and gestures that your child uses. **Imitate brushing teeth and yawning.**
Label	Name objects in your child's environment. **"Blanket" "Pillow"**
Expand	Add words to what your child says. **When your child says "Bed," you say, "Time for bed."**

Practice these important words and add more of your own:

TOOTHBRUSH	SLEEP	_____
TOOTHPASTE	BED	_____
BRUSH	BLANKET	_____
TEETH	PILLOW	_____
PAJAMAS	LIGHT	_____

BEDTIME

ACTIVITY IDEAS:
- When it is time for your child to brush his/her teeth, ask where things are as you look for them. (e.g., "Where is the toothbrush?" "On the sink!" "Where do you put the toothpaste?" "On the toothbrush!") Have your child point, use signs, words, or phrases to respond depending on his/her level.

- Talk about the steps we take when we go to bed. Draw pictures of what happens at bedtime and help your child put them in order. Talk about what is happening in each picture and encourage your child to talk about each step and label items they see. Use these pictures when your child is going to bed to show him/her what he/she needs to do and what is coming next.

I will help my child by:

- _____
- _____

My child will:

_____
_____
_____

THERAPIST SUGGESTS:

What happened?

-What did you do?
-What did your child say or do?
-What questions do you have?

_____
_____
_____

La Hora de Acostarse

12.2

Señalar	Junte señas y palabras. **Cama Dormir Cobija**
Ofrecer **M**odelos	Diga frases sencillas. **"A la cama" "Acuéstate"**
Nombrar	Nombre objetos en el ambiente. **"Cobija" "Almohada"**
Repetir	Repita sonidos, señas, palabras, y gestos que usa su niño/a.
Ímitar	**Imite a su niño/a en como se lava los dientes o como bosteza.**
Extender	Añada palabras a lo que dice su niño/a. **Cuando su niño/a diga "Cama," usted dígale, "A la cama."**

Practiquen estas palabras importantes y agreguen más:

CEPILLO	DORMIR	_____
PASTA	CAMA	_____
LAVARSE	COBIJA	_____
DIENTES	ALMOHADA	_____
PIJAMAS	LUZ	_____

La Hora de Acostarse

IDEAS DE ACTIVIDADES:
- Cuando llegue la hora de cepillarse los dientes, pregúntele a su niño/a dónde están las cosas que necesita mientras las busca. (por ejemplo, "¿Dónde está el cepillo de dientes?" "¡En el lavamanos!" "¿Dónde se pone la pasta dental?" "¡Sobre el cepillo de dientes!") Haga que su niño/a señale, use señas, palabras, o frases para responder, dependiendo de su nivel.

- Háblele acerca de los pasos que se siguen a la hora de dormir. Haga dibujos de lo que sucede a la hora de acostarse y ayude a su niño/a a ponerlos en orden. Explíquele lo que sucede en cada imagen y anime a su niño/a para que hable de cada paso y que le de nombres a lo que ve. Utilice esos dibujos cuando su niño/a vaya a acostarse para mostrarle lo que tiene que hacer y lo que viene despúes.

Ayudaré a mi niño/a así:

- _____
- _____

Mi niño/a va a:

_____
_____
_____

> SUGERENCIA DE LA TERAPISTA:

¿Qué pasó?
- ¿Qué hizo Ud.?
- ¿Qué dijo o hizo su niño/a?
- ¿Qué preguntas tiene Ud.?

_____
_____
_____

Bedtime/La Hora de Acostarse 12.3

Signs/Señas

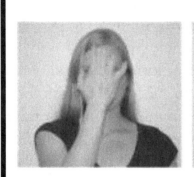 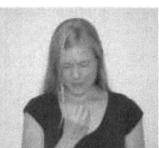

Sleep

Dormir

Bed

Cama

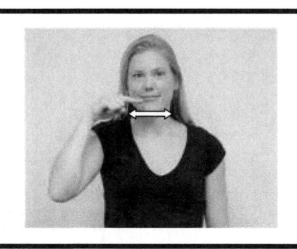

Brush teeth

Lavarse los dientes

Bedtime/La Hora de Acostarse

Blanket
Cobija

Turn on
Prender

Turn off
Apagar

Teaching how to follow directions 12.4

The ability to follow directions involves many skills. It requires a child to pay attention, understand what has been asked, remember what has been asked, and stop a task to complete the directions given to them. When we see that children are having difficulty following directions, it is important that we dissect just exactly what we are asking of them. Directions can range from very simple to quite complex. Often children are asked to do things that are over their head and they are viewed as being unsuccessful at following directions.

Educational plans often include goals that target understanding simple directions. A child needs to follow directions for her own safety as well as to reduce frustration. Unfortunately, children most frequently hear rapidly-fired commands in situations that demand an immediate response. These situations do not provide visual support and offer little time for teaching. While this is a necessary part of life for many students, other opportunities are needed to practice following directions in a more controlled setting. The events that take place throughout the day offer multiple chances to show a child how to properly follow directions. Most children enjoy participating in daily activities but can grow frustrated if they cannot participate or produce good work because they cannot follow directions.

Directions can be easily described as having a number of 1) steps and 2) components. Our instructions increase in difficulty as one or both of these aspects increase in number. Looking at the chart on the following page, you can see steady growth of an instruction as you add components. Make a copy of this chart and observe a student in a handful of settings to see where he is having the most success and where he is having difficulty. Once you know his level of functioning, share the information with his teacher to make her life easier and the child more successful. We can then choose to increase the demands by adding one step or one component. Count your tick marks in these boxes to serve as your data collection.

Additionally, you can record yourself as you teach and then count how many steps you include in your directions. Are there one, two, three, or four? How many components? Are your directions clear or confusing about what you expect children to do? Are their hidden or embedded instructions? When you say, "get ready to go" do you really mean clean up, grab your backpack, and get in line? It can be painful to listen to yourself but

Teaching how to follow directions

this is sometimes the quickest and most accurate way to do a correct self-assessment.

	1 Step	2 Steps	3 Steps
0 Components	Sit (or) Stand up	Stand up and get in line	Stand up, get in line, and don't move
1 Component	Touch your nose	Start walking and stop at the water fountain	Stop working, get in line and put on your coat
2 Components	Give me the blue square	Walk with your hands behind your back and stop in the hall	Stop working, put your things in your backpack, and get in line
3 Components	Touch the big red circle (from a group of red or big things)	Go to your table and sit in the yellow chair	Put your stuff in your desk, go to the door, and walk silently down the hall

Once we know our student's level of functioning in this area, there are plenty of opportunities to improve a child's ability to follow directions throughout the day. We begin by identifying why a child is not following directions. Is the problem behavior, or difficulty paying attention, understanding your language and directions, remembering them, or taking action? By figuring out the "why" we can get to the heart of the matter more quickly and offer specific support.

Suggestions to improve how a child follows directions:

1. **Give Warm-Up Clues** – Prior to giving the instruction, let the children know that they should be listening and ask if they are ready. "I am going to tell you what we are doing next. Eyes on me."

TEACHING HOW TO FOLLOW DIRECTIONS 12.4

2. **Use Visual and Auditory Clues** – Raise a sign, come up with a body movement or a call-and-response that clues the students into the fact that they are about to receive instructions. A few ideas that we have seen successful teachers use:
   - Put a large picture of an ear on the end of a stick that you raise when you are about to give instructions.
   - Play music or ring a bell
   - Use a clapping sequence. You clap twice and the children respond with three quick claps
   - You say "1, 2, 3, eyes on me." They respond "1, 2, eyes on you." This can be accompanied by pointing.
   - If you have a mascot, you yell the school name and the students yell the mascot. Teacher: "Bluebonnet" Students: "Bulldogs"
   - Use photos of children doing what you are asking them to do.

3. **Repeat the Instructions** – One way to guarantee that a child has heard you is to have her repeat the instruction before beginning the task. This also gives you great information about how many steps and components they are capable of remembering.

4. **Play Following Directions Game** – Games such as Simon Says, Red light Green Light, and Red Rover are great for teaching how to wait and follow instructions.

5. **Participate in Clean Up and Chores** – Ultimately, we all follow directions because we have a very concrete end in mind. We want to eat the cake we are baking. We want to use the piece of furniture that we are assembling. Tie following directions to an outcome that is observable and has an immediate impact, such as cleaning up a room.

Following Directions Activity
Bedtime/La hora de acostarse

Teach your child how to follow directions by having him/her get ready for bed.

Enseñe a su niño/a como seguir instrucciones al pedir que se prepare para acostarse.

Time for bed!
¡Es la hora de acostarse!

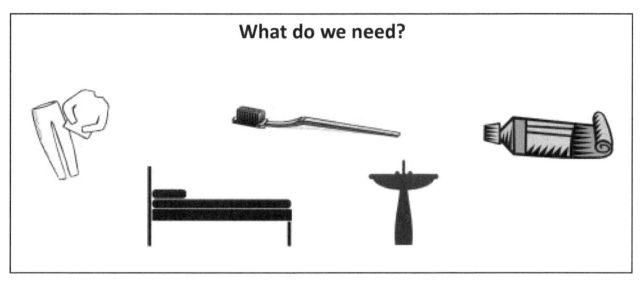

What do we need?

Directions / Las instrucciones	What did your child do/say? / ¿Qué dijo/hizo su niño/a?
Take off clothes / Quítate la ropa	
Put on pajamas / Ponte el pijama	
Brush your teeth / Lávate los dientes	
Pick out a book / Escoge un libro	
Get into bed / Acuéstate	
Read the book / Lee el libro	
Say goodnight / Di buenas noches	

Appendix

FACT OR MYTH?
FAQs about Bilingual Language Development

1. **Myth**: Children code-switch between languages because they don't know either language well.

   Fact: Actually, it is a normal developmental process to code-switch between languages (Genesee et al., 2004; Nocoladis & Secco, 2000). Sometimes bilinguals intentionally switch languages for effect, similar to mixing jargon or slang in standard speech (Langdon, 2008). Additionally, research shows that children who are raised in bilingual environments typically express 70% of their concepts in one language or the other and only 30% in both languages (Pearson, Fernandez, & Oller, 1995; Peña, Bedore, & Zlatic, 2002). When we look at skills across both languages, a bilingual child reaches similar language milestones and has a vocabulary that is comparable in size to a monolingual child (Pearson, 1993; Pearson and Fernandez, 2001).

2. **Myth**: Raising children with two languages will confuse them.

   Fact: Research indicates that exposure to multiple languages does **not** have a negative impact on speech acquisition (sound production) or language acquisition (words and word combinations) (Goldstein, 2004; Bialystock, 2009). Children who learn two languages in a supportive, language-rich environment can learn both languages well.

3. **Myth**: Parents should not use more than one language with their child.

   Fact: Parents should choose a method that feels comfortable to them, as that is the one that will likely result in the greatest success. The thing to keep in mind is that the amount a child *hears* a language drives the amount a child *uses* a language.

4. **Myth**: The preferred method of learning a second language in the home is to have one person speak one language and one person speak the other language.

   Fact: The method of *One Parent One Language* is only one style of raising a bilingual child. Every family is different, therefore the language delivery in each home will vary and that is okay! Children learn to differentiate between the languages spoken to them. Research points out that there is no evidence that mixing languages negatively affects language acquisition in children with typical development or in children with delayed or atypical language development (Buckley, 2002; Dopke, 2006; Goldstein, 2004; Peña, 2011).

5. **Myth**: Children with language impairments should not learn more than one language at a time.

   Fact: Research indicates that it is not detrimental for children with speech and language delays to learn two languages in a bilingual environment (Paradis, 2007). Bilingual children who have speech and language impairments typically demonstrate similar problems in both of their languages (Paradis, Crago, & Genesee, 2006). This does not mean that they are unable to communicate in both languages or that they are confused because they are hearing two languages.

   Consider your child's ability to learn language. If they can easily learn language, then teaching them two languages will likely be successful; if they struggle, then you may reconsider teaching them two languages if it is not something already happening in their daily life.

6. **Myth**: The optimum time for learning two languages is before the age of three.

   Fact: Exposure to the language is what is required. Many children (and adults) can acquire a new language at any time in their lives if they are exposed to it on a regular basis. Learning a new language is not limited to children below age three (McLaughlin, 1984).

See www.nethelp.no/cindy/myth.html and www.spanglishbaby.com for responses to many myths about bilingualism.

Apples To Apples

The following milestones are expected for all children, regardless of home language.

Building Blocks for Speech

0-1 month – crying and vegetative sounds

1-6 months – cooing, laughter, squealing, growling

4-6 months – marginal babbling

6-8 months – reduplicated babbling

8-10 months – variegated babbling

8-12 months – echolalia

9-12 months – phonetically consistent forms

9-12 months – jargon

Speech Intelligibility

For parents: (Lynch, Brookshire & Fox, 1980)

    18 months - ~25% intelligible

    2 year olds - 50-75% intelligible

    3 year olds - 75%-100% intelligible

For unfamiliar listener: (Flipsen, 2006)

    18 months - ~25% intelligible

    2 year olds - ~50% intelligible

    3 year olds - ~75% intelligible

    4 year olds - 100% intelligible

Common Consonant Inventories in English & Spanish

Age	#	Inventory (E&S, **E**, *S*)
12 M	5	b d g m **h**
18 M	9	b d m n w s **h t** *y*
24 M	10	b d p t k m n s w **h** *y*
30 M	13	b d p t k m n s w g f **h** *y*
36 M	13	b d p t k m n s w g f *y* **h**

Building Blocks for Language

0-1 month – crying and vegetative sounds

2-3 months – eye gaze

6-9 months – joint attention

9-12 months – using gestures

12-15 months – following simple commands

18 months – symbolic play, pretend play

24 months – sequencing of activities

36 months – episodic play

Language Trajectories

Bilingual children develop early vocabulary at the same rate as monolingual children (Pearson, Fernández, & Oller, 1993; Umbel et al., 1992).

Early language milestones are similar (single words, lexical spurt, 2-word phrases) (Pearson and Fernández, 1994).

Conceptual scores are similar (Pearson, 1998; Kester, & Peña, 2002; Bedore, et al. 2005).

Vocabulary Development

12 months – first words (usually labeling familiar objects, and actions in child's environment)

15 months – 4-6 word vocabulary

18 months – 20-50 word vocabulary

24 months – 200-300 word vocabulary

36 months - roughly 1000 words

Overextensions (e.g., calling all men 'Dada')

Underextensions (e.g., calling a tiger 'kitty')

Routines-Based Early Intervention Guidebook

STRATEGIES FOR SPEECH PRODUCTION

SAY & CUE	Pair movements, touch, and visuals with specific sounds. **Point to lips when saying "b."** **Slide finger down arm when saying "s" in "spoon."**
MODEL	Emphasize specific sounds by breaking words apart. **"b-b-b-ball" "mmmmama" "ba-na-na"**
IMITATE	Repeat what your child says, but with emphasis on correct sounds. **If your child says "tao," repeat, "Yes, it's a cow."**
LABEL	Label items in your child's environment that begin with the same sound. **"Let's find things that begin with 'b'…ball, baby, bubble, banana."**
EXPAND	Once your child can say a specific sound by itself, practice the sound in syllables, then words, phrases, sentences, and finally in conversation. **"b" …. "ba" … "baby" … "my baby" … "The baby is sleeping."**
SEÑALAR	Acompañe sonidos específicos con movimientos, apoyos visuales y el sentido del tacto. **Señale los labios mientras dice "b."** **Deslice un dedo sobre su brazo mientras dice "s" en "escuela."**
OFRECER MODELOS	Separe palabras para dar énfasis a sonidos específicos. **"b-b-b-bebé" "mmmmamá" "pe-lo-ta"**
NOMBRAR	Nombre objetos en el ambiente de su niño que empiecen con el mismo sonido. **"Vamos a buscar cosas que empiecen con 'b'…bloque, bebé, boca."**
REPETIR	Repita lo que dice su niño, pero con énfasis en los sonidos correctos. **Si su niño dice "tayó," repita "Sí, se cayó."**
ÍMITAR	
EXTENDER	Una vez que su niño pueda decir un sonido específico por sí mismo, practique el sonido en sílabas, luego en palabras, frases, oraciones y, finalmente, en conversaciones. **"b" …. "be" … "bebé" … "mi bebé" … "El bebé está durmiendo."**

Routines-Based Early Intervention Guidebook

SPEECH DEVELOPMENT

Sound	Birth - 3 Years	3 - 4 Years	4 - 5 Years
m	S (full) / E (to ~3)		
n	S (full) / E (to ~3)		
p	S (full) / E (to ~3)		
b	S (full) / E (to ~3)		
t	S (full to 4) / E (full to 3)		
d	S (full) / E (to ~3)		
k	S (full) / E (to ~3)		
g	S (full to 5) / E (to ~3)		
f	S (full to ~4) / E (to ~3)		
ð	S → (beyond 5) / E → (beyond 5)		
s	S → (beyond 5) / E → (beyond 5)		
tʃ	S (full to 5) / E (full to 5)		
l	S (full to 5) / E → (beyond 5)		

Each bar indicates that a sound is developing but may not yet be mastered. Arrows indicate continued development of the sound beyond age 5.

S = Spanish
E = English

Speech Development

	Birth - 3 Years	3 - 4 Years	4 - 5 Years

English Only

ŋ	E———————————————→		
h	E——→		
w	E——→		
v	E———————————————→		
θ	E———————————————→		
z	E———————————————→		
ʃ	E———————————————→		
ʒ	E———————————————→		
dʒ	E———————————————→		
ɹ	E———————————————→		

Spanish Only

x	S———————————————→		
ɲ	S———————————————→		
ɾ	S———————————————→		
r	S———————————————→		

Acevedo, 1993; Bedore, 1999; Goldstein and Iglesias, 2006; Jimenez, 1987; Goldman-Fristoe Test of Articulation-2nd Edition, 2000; Iowa-Nebraska Study, 1990

Routines-Based Early Intervention Guidebook

PHONOLOGICAL DEVELOPMENT

	2 - 3 Years	3 - 4 Years	4 - 5 Years

Syllabic Patterns in English and Spanish

Process	2-3 Years	3-4 Years	4-5 Years
Final Consonant Deletion	S		
	E		
Medial Consonant Deletion	S		
	E	E	E
Initial Consonant Deletion	S		
	E		
Weak Syllable Deletion	S		
	E	E	
Cluster Reduction	S		
	E	E	

Substitution Patterns in English and Spanish

Process	2-3 Years	3-4 Years	4-5 Years
Stopping	S		
	E		
Fronting	S		
	E	E	
Liquid Simplification	S		
	E →	E →	E →
Gliding	S		
	E →	E →	E →
Assimilation	S		
	E		
Backing	S		
	E		
Vocalization	E →	E →	E →
Flap/Trill Deviation	S →	S →	S →

Each bar indicates the acceptable age range for use of the process. Arrows indicate continued use of the process beyond age 5.

S = Spanish   E = English

Goldstein and Iglesias, 2006; Grunwell, 1982; Shriberg, 1993

TYPICAL PHONOLOGICAL PROCESSES

Suppressed by age:		Pattern	English Example	Spanish Example
English (Shriberg)	Spanish (Goldstein+)	**Syllabic Patterns**		
3	3 (uncommon)	Initial Consonant Deletion	"at" for "cat"	"ato" for "gato"
3	3	Final Consonant Deletion	"ca" for "cat"	"sa" for "sal"
4	3	Weak Syllable Deletion	"telphone" for "telephone"	"fermo" for "enfermo"
4	3	Medial Consonant Deletion	"ta_o" for "taco"	"ta_o" for "taco"
4	5	Cluster Reduction	"fat" for "flat"	"faco" for "flaco"
7	5	Gliding	"bwack" for "black"	"peyo" for "pelo"
		Substitution Patterns		
3	3	Assimilation	"tato" for "taco"	"tato" for "taco"
3	3	Backing	"kat" for "bat"	"kate" for "bate"
3	5	Stopping	"bat" for "fat"	"capé" for "café"
4	3	Fronting	"bat" for "kat"	"bota" for "boca"
7	5	Liquid Simplification	"wake" for "lake"	"peyo" for "pelo"
7	NA	Vocalization	"powah" for "power"	
NA	5	Flap/Trill Deviation		"datón" for "ratón"

Bedore, 2007; Fabiano and Goldstein, 2010; Goldstein and Iglesias, 2006; Shriberg, 1993

Routines-Based Early Intervention Guidebook

LANGUAGE MILESTONES

RECEPTIVE LANGUAGE

0 - 6 Months
- Moves eyes toward direction of sound
- Reacts to loud noises

6 - 12 Months
- Recognizes familiar objects when named
- Understands "no"

1 - 2 Years
- Points to named items in book/picture
- Listens to short stories for several minutes
- Points to familiar body parts
- Follows simple commands
- Engages in symbolic play

→ AGE

EXPRESSIVE LANGUAGE

0 - 6 Months
- Vocalizes discomfort, pleasure

6 - 12 Months
- Babbles ("ma-ma-ma")
- Uses gestures

1 - 2 Years
- Uses early consonants (m,p,b) and most vowels
- Says 1-2 words phrases
- Begins to make environmental noises
- Begins to respond to questions with gestures and pointing

Both English and Spanish | English Only | Spanish Only

Routines-Based Early Intervention Guidebook

LANGUAGE MILESTONES

2 - 3 YEARS

- Follows 2-step directives
- Responds to Yes/No Questions

- Uses regular past tense and simple preterit
- Produces speech that is often easy to understand
- Uses more consonants in speech (t,d,g,k)
- Begins use of plural form
- Uses present progressive verb forms
- Combines 2-3 words to comment and inquire
- **Uses correct article gender**
- **Uses indefinite/ definite articles**

3 - 4 YEARS

- Answers simple "WH" Questions
- Engages in episodic play

- Combines 4+ words
- Uses possessives
- Uses irregular past tense, imperfect, and preterit
- Shares personal experiences (school, friends) in short personal narratives
- Begins to describe objects use
- Produces speech that is easy to understand most of the time
- Generally speaks easily without effort in initiating sounds
- Uses negatives
- Uses indefinite/definite articles

4 - 5 YEARS

- Follows 3-step directions

- Uses adjectives
- Uses the same grammar as family/home environment
- Produces most consonant sounds present in language
- Tells a story related to a topic

Goldstein, 1990; Hulit and Howard, 2006; Kester, et al., 2010; Paul, 2001; Rosetti, 2006; Typical Speech and Language Development, 1997-2011; Wein, 2007; Zimmerman, et al., 2002; Zimmerman, et al., 2002

INDEX OF SIGNS - ENGLISH

Again	156
All done	22
Baby	73
Bag	115
Ball	73
Bed	170
Blanket	171
Blocks	73
Book	156
Brush teeth	170
Bubbles	142
Car	100
Clean up	128
Close	157
Cold	143
Come	101
Cookie	47
Dad	32
Diaper	61
Dog	87
Down	114
Drink	46
Duck	142
Eat	46
Fell down	72
Flowers	87
Get dressed	60
Hat	61
Hello/Bye	33
Help	23
Hot	143
House	100
Hug	33
I want	23
Inside	129
Juice	47

Word	Page
Jump	86
Kiss	33
Let's go	101
Milk	47
Mom	32
Money	115
More	22
Music	143
My turn	72
On	129
Open	157
Pants	60
Plane	100
Play	72
Please	22
Put	115
See	157
Shirt	61
Shoes	60
Sit	128
Sleep	170
Stand	128
Stop	101
Store	114
Swing	86
Television	129
Throw	87
Thank you	23
Tree	86
Turn page	156
Turn off	171
Turn on	171
Up	114
Wash	142
Water	46
Where	32

Index of Signs - Spanish/Índice de Señas

Abajo	114
Abrazo	33
Abrir	157
Adentro	129
Agua	46
Apagar	171
Árbol	86
Arriba	114
Avión	100
Ayuda	23
Bebé	73
Beber	46
Beso	33
Bloques	73
Bolsa	115
Brincar	86
Burbujas	142
Caliente	143
Cama	170
Cambiar la página	156
Camisa	61
Carro	100
Casa	100
Cerrar	157
Cobija	171
Columpio	86
Comer	46
Dinero	115
Dónde	32
Dormir	170
En	129
Flores	87
Frío	143
Galleta	47
Gorra	61
Gracias	23

Hola/Adiós	33
Jugar	72
Jugo	47
Lavarse	142
Lavarse los dientes	170
Leche	47
Levantarse	128
Libro	156
Limpiar	128
Mamá	32
Más	22
Mi turno	72
Música	143
Otra vez	156
Pañal	61
Pantalones	60
Papá	32
Parar	101
Pato	142
Pelota	73
Perro	87
Poner	115
Por favor	22
Prender	171
Quiero	23
Se acabó	22
Se cayó	72
Sentarse	128
Televisión	129
Tienda	114
Tirar	87
Vámonos	101
Venir	101
Ver	157
Vestirse	60
Zapatos	60

REFERENCES

Acevedo, M.A. (1993). Development of Spanish consonants in preschool children. *Journal of Childhood Communication Disorders, 15,* 9–15.

Bedore, L. (1999). The Acquisition of Spanish. In O. Taylor & L. Leonard (Eds.), *Language acquisition across North America: Cross-cultural and cross-linguistic perspectives* (pp. 157-208). San Diego: Singular Publishing Group.

Bedore, L. M., Peña, E. D., García, M., & Cortez, C. (2005). Conceptual versus monolingual scoring: When does it make a difference? Speech, Language, Hearing Services in Schools, 36, 188-200.

Bialystok, E. (2009). Bilingualism: The Good, the Bad, and the Indifferent. *Bilingualism: Language and Cognition, 12,* 1, 3-11.

Buckley, S.J. (2002). Can Children with Down Syndrome Learn More than One Language? *Down Syndrome News and Update, 2,* 3, 100-102.

Davis, B.L., Bedore, L. (2007). *Developmental Speech Disorders.* San Diego, CA: Plural Publishing Inc.

Dopke, S. (2006). Is Bilingualism Detrimental for Children with Autism? Retrieved October 13, 2011 from http://www.bilingualoptions.com.au/consTXTAutism.pdf.

Fabiano-Smith, L., Goldstein, B.A. (2010). Early-, Middle-, and Late-Developing Sounds in Monolingual and Bilingual Children: An Exploratory Investigation. *American Journal of Speech-Language Pathology, 19,* 66-77.

Flipsen, P., Jr. (2006). Measuring the intelligibility of conversational speech in children. *Clinical Linguistics and Phonetics. 20,* 4, 202-312.

Genesee, F., Paradis, J., & Crago, M. (2004). Dual-language Development and Disorders: A Handbook on Bilingualism and Second Language Learning. Baltimore, MD: Paul H. Brookes Publishing Co.

Goldman, R., Fristoe, M. (2000). *Goldman-Fristoe Test of Articulation.* Circle Pines, MN: American Guidance Service.

Goldstein, B. (1990). *Cultural and Linguistic Diversity Resource Guide for Speech Language Pathologists.* New York, Singular Publishing Group, Inc.

Goldstein, B. (2004). *Bilingual Language Development and Disorders in Spanish-English Speakers.* Baltimore, MD: Paul H. Brookes Publishing Co.

Goldstein, B., Iglesias, A. (2006). *Contextual Probes of Articulation Competence-Spanish.* Greenville, SC: Super Duper Publications.

Goodwyn, Acredolo, & Brown (2000). Impact of symbolic gesturing on early language development. *Journal of Nonverbal Behavior, 24,* 81-103.

Grunwell, P. (1982). *Clinical Phonology* (p. 183). Rockville, MD: Aspen Systems Corporation.

REFERENCES

Hulit, L. M., Howard, M.R. (2006). Born to talk: An introduction to speech and language development, Fourth Edition. Boston, MA: Allyn & Bacon.

Jimenez, B.C. (1987). Acquisition of Spanish consonants in children aged 3-5 years, 7 months. *Language, Speech, and Hearing Services in the Schools*, 18 (4), 357-363.

Kester, E., Prath, S., Wirka, M., & Lebel, K. (2010, October 11). Typical Development in Bilinguals. Bilingual Assessment and Intervention. Presented at Education Service Center Region XIII. Austin, TX.

Kester, E.S. & Peña, Elizabeth D. (2002). Language ability assessment of Spanish-English bilinguals: future directions. Practical Assessment, Research & Evaluation, 8(4).

Kummerer, B., Lopez-Reyna, N.A., & Hughes, M.T. (2007). Mexican Immigrant Mothers' Perceptions of Their Children's Communication Disabilities, Emergent Literacy Development, and Speech-Language Therapy Program. *American Journal of Speech-Language Pathology, 16*, 271-282.

Langdon, H. (2008). Assessment & Intervention for Communication Disorders in Culturally & Linguistically Diverse Populations. Clifton Park: Delmar.

Lynch, J.I., Brookshire, B.L., & Fox, D.R. (1980). *A Parent - Child Cleft Palate Curriculum: Developing Speech and Language*. OR: CC Publications.

McLaughlin, B. (1984). *Second-language acquisition in childhood: Vol. 1 Preschool children* (2nd ed.). Hillsdale, JK: Lawrence Erlbaum.

McWilliams, R. (2007). Early Intervention in Natural Environments. Retrieved February 5, 2008 from http://naturalenvironments.blogspot.com/2007/10/toy-bags.html

Nicoladis, E. & Secco, G. (2000). The Role of a Child's Productive Vocabulary in the Language Choice of a Bilingual Family. *First Language, 58,* 3-28.

Paradis, J., Crago, M., & Genesee, F. (2006). Domain-general versus domain-specific accounts of specific language impairment: Evidence from bilingual children's acquisition of object pronouns. *Language Acquisition,13*, 33 – 62.

Paradis, J. (2007a). Bilingual children with specific language impairment: Theoretical and applied issues. *Applied Psycholinguistics, 28,* 551 – 564.

Pearson, B.Z. (1998). Assessing lexical development in bilingual babies and toddlers. *International Journal of Bilingualism, 2,* 347-372.

Pearson, B.Z., & Fernández, S.C. (1994). Patterns of interaction in the lexical development in two languages of bilingual infants. *Language Learning, 44,* 617-653.

Pearson, B., Fernández, S.C., Lewedag, V., & Oller, D.K. (1997). Input factors in lexical learning of bilingual infants (ages 10 – 30 months). *Applied Psycholinguistics, 18*, 41- 58.

REFERENCES

Pearson, B.Z., Fernández, S.C., & Oller, D.K., (1993). Lexical development in bilingual infants and toddlers: Comparison to monolingual norms. *Language Learning, 43*, 93-120.

Pearson, B.Z., Fernández, S., & Oller, D.K. (1995). Cross-language synonyms in the lexicons of bilingual infants: One language or two? *Journal of Child Language, 22,* 345-368.

Peña, E.D., Bedore, L.M., & Zlatic-Giunta, R. (2002). Category generation performance of young bilingual children: The influence of condition, category, and language. *Journal of Speech-Language, and Hearing Research*, *41,* 938-947.

Peña, E.D. (2011). Bilingualism Does NOT Increase Risk for Language Impairment. Retrieved October 13, 2011 from http://2languages2worlds.wordpress.com.

Pizer, G., Walters, K., & Meier, R.P. (2007). Bringing up baby with baby signs: Language ideologies and socialization in hearing families. *Sign Language Studies, 7* (4), 387-430.

Rogoff, B. (1990). Apprenticeship in Thinking. Oxford: Oxford University Press.

Rosetti, L. (2006). The Rosetti infant-toddler language scale. East Moline, IL: LinguiSystems, Inc.

Paul, R. (2001). *Language disorders from infancy through adolescence: Assessment and intervention*. St. Louis, MO: Mosby, Inc..

Shriberg, L. (1993). Four new speech and prosody-voice measures for genetics research and other studies in developmental phonological disorders. *Journal of Speech and Hearing Research, 36*, 105-140.

Thompson, R.H., Cotnoir-Bichelman, N.M., McKerchar, P.M., Tate, T.L., & Dancho, K.A. (2007). Enhancing early communication through infant sign training. *Journal of Applied Behavior Analysis, 40*, 15-23.

Typical Speech and Language Development (1997-2011). American Speech-Language Hearing Association. Retrieved August 2, 2011 from http://www.asha.org/public/speech/development/.

Umbel, V.M., Pearson, B.Z., Fernández, M.C., & Oller, D.K. (1992). Measuring bilingual children's receptive vocabularies. Child Development, 63, 1012-1020.

Vygotsky, L.S. (1967). Play and its role in the mental development of the child. *Soviet Psychology, 5*, 6-18.

Wein, H., (September 2007). Is Baby Babbling on Schedule? *News in Health.* Retrieved August 2, 2011 from http://newsinhealth.nih.gov/2007/September/docs/01features_01.htm

Zimmerman, I.L., Steiner, V.G., & Pond, R.E. (2002). *Preschool language scales-4th edition*. San Antonio, TX: The Psychological Corporation.

Zimmerman, I.L., Steiner, V.G., & Pond, R.E. (2002). *Preschool language scales-4th edition Spanish*. San Antonio, TX: The Psychological Corporation.